CGP makes Spanish grammar simple!

Addled by adverbs? Puzzled by prepositions?
Never fear — this CGP Handbook is here to save the day.

It's packed with crystal-clear notes explaining all the grammar you'll need to triumph in GCSE 9-1 Spanish.

With CGP, turn your grammar siestas into grammar fiestas!

CGP — still número uno! ☺

Our sole aim here at CGP is to produce the highest quality books — carefully written, immaculately presented and dangerously close to being funny.

Then we work our socks off to get them out to you
— at the cheapest possible prices.

Contents

Section 1 — Nouns and Articles

Using Nouns 2
Masculine and Feminine Nouns 3
Plural Nouns 4
Articles 5

Section 2 — Pronouns

Using Pronouns 7
Subject Pronouns 8
Tú and Usted 9
Direct Object Pronouns 10
Indirect Object Pronouns 11
Ordering Pronouns 12
Relative Pronouns 14
Interrogative Pronouns 16
Possessive Pronouns 17
Demonstrative Pronouns 18

Section 3 — Adjectives

Using Adjectives 19
Adjective Agreement 20
Adjective Position 22
Indefinite Adjectives 25
Interrogative Adjectives 26
Demonstrative Adjectives 27
Possessive and Relative Adjectives 28
Comparative Adjectives 30
Superlative Adjectives 31

Section 4 — Adverbs

Using Adverbs 32
Useful Adverbs 33
Other Useful Adverbs 34
Adverbial Phrases 35
Quantifiers and Intensifiers 36
Comparative and Superlative Adverbs 37

Section 5 — Verbs

Using Verbs ... 38
Infinitives ... 41
Present Tense — Regular Verbs ... 42
Present Tense — Verb Endings ... 43
Radical-Changing Verbs ... 44
Irregular Verbs ... 45
'Ser' and 'Estar' ... 46
Reflexive Verbs ... 48
Preterite vs. Imperfect ... 50
Preterite Tense — Regular Verbs ... 51
Preterite Tense — Irregular Verbs ... 52
Imperfect Tense ... 54
Perfect Tense ... 56
Past Participles ... 57
Pluperfect Tense ... 58
Immediate Future Tense ... 59
Proper Future Tense ... 60
Conditional Tense ... 61
Verbs with '-ing' ... 62
Negatives ... 64
Passive ... 66
Impersonal Verbs ... 67
Subjunctive ... 68
Imperfect Subjunctive ... 71
Imperative ... 72
Asking Questions ... 74

Section 6 — Other Useful Stuff

Numbers ... 75
Dates, Days and Time ... 76
Conjunctions ... 77
Prepositions ... 79
'Por' and 'Para' ... 81

Index ... 82

Published by CGP

Editors: Sian Butler, Heather Cowley, Gabrielle Richardson and Hannah Roscoe

With thanks to Rose Jones and Encarna Aparicio-Dominguez for the proofreading.

ISBN: 978 1 78908 261 6

Clipart from Corel®

Printed by Elanders Ltd, Newcastle upon Tyne.

Based on the classic CGP style created by Richard Parsons.

Text, design, layout and original illustrations
© Coordination Group Publications Ltd. (CGP) 2020
All rights reserved.

Photocopying more than one section of this book is not permitted, even if you have a CLA licence.
Extra copies are available from CGP with next day delivery • 0800 1712 712 • www.cgpbooks.co.uk

Section 1 — Nouns and Articles

The Essentials

Using Nouns

You'll find nouns in most sentences, so getting to grips with them is crucial.

1. Nouns are words for things

1) Nouns are words that name stuff like people, places and things:

   crab   Chile   surprise   January   Hector

2) Nouns can be singular or plural: singular   plural

   frog ⟶ frogs

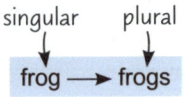

3) In Spanish, nouns are also masculine or feminine:

   masculine ⟶ **el conejo** — the rabbit   feminine ⟶ **la camiseta** — the T-shirt

4) When you learn a Spanish noun, it's really important to learn its gender too.

5) See p.3 for how to tell masculine and feminine nouns apart.

2. Articles are words like 'a', 'an' and 'the'

1) Articles are little words that go before nouns, like 'the', 'a' or 'an'.

2) 'A' and 'an' are used for general things — they're indefinite articles:

   a dog   'A dog' is talking about a dog in general, not a specific dog.

3) 'The' is used to talk about something specific — it's the definite article:

   the dog   'The dog' refers to a specific dog.

4) In Spanish, the article can usually help you identify the gender of a noun.

5) See p.5-6 for definite and indefinite articles in Spanish.

Masculine and Feminine Nouns

Every Spanish noun is masculine or feminine

The gender of a Spanish noun is really important — it affects things like which version of the article to use, or how to spell an adjective.

masculine → **el conejo negro** — the black rabbit
feminine → **la camiseta negra** — the black T-shirt
definite article (p.5)   adjective (p.19)

'El' or 'un' in front of a noun usually means it's masculine.
'La' or 'una' in front of a noun usually means it's feminine.

It's no use just learning the noun — you need to learn its gender too.

Use these general rules to help you

You might not always know whether a noun is masculine or feminine. You can use these general rules to help you work out the gender of the noun. But be careful — not all nouns follow these rules.

1) Masculine nouns often end in these letter patterns:

   -o   -l   -n   -r
   -s   -ta   -aje

   Also masculine: male people, languages, days, months, seas, rivers, oceans and mountains.

2) Feminine nouns tend to end in these letter patterns:

   -a   -ción   -sión   -tad
   -tud   -dad   -umbre

   Also feminine: female people and letters of the alphabet.

Learn these irregular nouns

1) For nouns ending in '-e' or '-ista', you can't tell if they're masculine or feminine, so you just have to learn them.

   el coche — car
   la gente — people
   el turista / la turista — tourist (m) / tourist (f)

Shanice's new motorbike was a bit irregular.

2) There are also other irregulars that you'll have to learn:

   el día — day
   el mapa — map
   el problema — problem
   la mano — hand
   la foto — photo
   la moto — motorbike

Section 1 — Nouns and Articles

Plural Nouns

It's easy to make some Spanish nouns plural, but others can be trickier. Take a look at this page to help you deal with all different types of nouns.

Add an '-s' to most nouns

1) You make most Spanish nouns plural by adding an '-s':

   el barco — los barcos   un barco — unos barcos
   the boat — the boats   a boat — some boats

2) When you make a noun plural, don't forget to make the article plural. See p.5-6.

   el ⟶ los   la ⟶ las   uno ⟶ unos   una ⟶ unas

EXCEPTIONS

1) Some words follow a different rule. Here are the most common ones:

Noun ending	Irregular plural ending	Example
consonants except 'z'	-es	el color (colour) ⟶ los colores
-z	-ces	la voz (voice) ⟶ las voces

2) Days of the week that end in '-s' don't change their ending in the plural — you just need to change the article:

   el martes ⟶ los martes

3) To make surnames plural, make the article plural but keep the noun the same: Los Taylor — The Taylors

Accents sometimes change in the plural

Occasionally, you might need to add or remove an accent from a noun to avoid changing the pronunciation of a word in the plural:

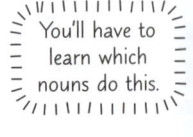

You'll have to learn which nouns do this.

   el inglés — an Englishman ⟶ los ingleses — the Englishmen

   el joven — the young man ⟶ los jóvenes — the young men

Section 1 — Nouns and Articles

Articles

Articles are the little words that come before nouns, like 'a', 'an' and 'the'.
Make sure you know the difference between definite and indefinite articles:

> Definite articles refer to a specific thing, e.g. the horse.
> Indefinite articles refer to general things, e.g. a horse.

'El', 'la', 'los' and 'las' are definite articles

1) The word for 'the' changes in Spanish depending on the gender of the noun and whether it's singular or plural:

	masculine	feminine
singular	el	la
plural	los	las

EXCEPTIONS

For feminine nouns beginning with a stressed 'a', you need to use 'el':

el aula — the classroom

el agua — the water

2) You can use the neuter article 'lo' for things that don't have a gender.

lo bueno — the good thing
lo malo — the bad thing

When you use 'lo' before an adjective, the adjective has to be in the masculine form.

Spanish uses definite articles differently

Sometimes you need to use a definite article in Spanish where you wouldn't in English. Remember to use them with:

nouns used in a general sense	→ Me encanta la música	(I love music)
days of the week and times	→ los domingos a las nueve	(on Sundays at 9 o'clock)
weights and measurements	→ cinco libras el kilo	(five pounds per kilo)
a person's title	→ La señora Díaz	(Mrs Díaz)

Articles

'A' and 'de' change before definite articles

1) When you use 'a' (to) or 'de' (of / from) with the masculine form of the definite article, don't say 'de el' or 'a el'.

2) 'A' and 'de' combine with 'el' to make new words:

   a + el = al ⟶ **Voy al polideportivo.**
   — I go to the sports centre.

   de + el = del ⟶ **Vivo cerca del campo.**
   — I live close to the countryside.

'Un', 'una', 'unos' and 'unas' are indefinite articles

1) There are different ways of saying 'a' in Spanish.
   Use 'un' for masculine words and 'una' for feminine words:

   un pastel — a cake   **una uva** — a grape

2) In the plural form, indefinite articles are used to mean 'some' or 'a few':

   unos pasteles — some cakes   **unas uvas** — some grapes

You don't always need to include the article

1) The indefinite article isn't included when using 'ser' + occupation or nationality:

   Es bombera. — She's a firefighter.

   Es alemán. — He's German.

2) It's not used after a negative verb:

   No tengo chaqueta. — I don't have a jacket.

Jimena didn't fight fire — she embraced it.

Section 1 — Nouns and Articles

Section 2 — Pronouns

The Essentials: Using Pronouns

If you liked nouns, it's about to get even more exciting — welcome to pronouns.

1. Pronouns are words that replace nouns

1) Pronouns are little words like 'you', 'she' and 'they'. You can use a pronoun in place of a noun so that you don't have to keep repeating it.

> The shoes are yellow and **they** are spotty.
> ↳ Use '<u>they</u>' instead of repeating '<u>the shoes</u>'.

2) Subject (personal) pronouns replace the subject of a sentence — see p.8. They change depending on who in the sentence is doing the action.

> **He** read the book.
> ↳ '<u>He</u>' is <u>doing</u> the action.
>
> **We** played outside.
> ↳ '<u>We</u>' are <u>doing</u> the action.

3) Object pronouns replace objects in a sentence — see p.10-11.
The direct object is the person or thing having the action done to it.
The indirect object is often a person that follows 'to', 'for' or 'by'.

> **Jack** made a **cake** for **Claude**. — indirect object
> ↳ subject ↳ direct object
>
> Jack made **it** for **him**. — indirect object pronoun
> ↑ direct object pronoun

2. There are more types of pronouns

1) Relative pronouns introduce more information about a noun — see p.14-15.

> I met someone **who** was very friendly. ← '<u>Who</u>' introduces a relative clause with more information about the person they met.

2) Interrogative pronouns are used to ask questions — see p.16.

> **What** did she promise you?

3) Possessive pronouns show who owns something — see p.17.

> Those glasses are **yours**.

4) 'This' and 'that' are demonstrative pronouns — see p.18.

> **This** is really good fun.

Subject Pronouns

Subject pronouns replace nouns

1) In English, you use a subject pronoun to replace the subject (main person / thing doing the action) in a sentence.

> Kat realised there was a mistake. **She** corrected it.

'She' is used instead of repeating 'Kat'.

2) You don't normally include subject pronouns in Spanish sentences because verb endings show you who is doing the action — but you still need to know them.

Luciana made sure all her subjects knew they were replaceable.

Learn the Spanish subject pronouns

I	**yo**	we	**nosotros/as**
you (informal singular)	**tú**	you (informal plural)	**vosotros/as**
he / it	**él**	they (masc. or masc. & fem.)	**ellos**
she / it	**ella**	they (feminine)	**ellas**
you (formal singular)	**usted**	you (formal plural)	**ustedes**

EXCEPTIONS

1) Although you don't usually need subject pronouns in Spanish, they are used when you want to emphasise exactly who does what:

> **Yo** quiero jugar al fútbol, pero **él** quiere nadar.
> — **I** want to play football, but **he** wants to swim.

The pronouns are used in Spanish when extra stress is put on pronouns in English.

2) The verb endings for 'he' and 'she' are the same, so subject pronouns can be used to make the meaning of a sentence clear.

> **Él lee** una revista y **ella lee** el periódico.
> — **He** reads a magazine and **she** reads the newspaper.

Section 2 — Pronouns

Tú and Usted

'Tú' and 'usted' — Informal and Formal 'you'

1) In Spanish, there are four different ways of saying 'you'.

informal singular	informal plural	formal singular	formal plural
tú	vosotros/as	usted	ustedes

2) They each go with a different part of the verb. 'Usted' and 'ustedes' don't use the same 'you' part of the verb as 'tú' and 'vosotros':

- For 'usted', use the 'he/she/it' part of the verb.
- For 'ustedes', use the 'they' part of the verb.

3) Here are the four different ways of asking where someone is going:

¿Adónde vas? — tú   **¿Adónde va?** — usted

¿Adónde vais? — vosotros/as   **¿Adónde van?** — ustedes

Choosing the correct 'you'

1) The one you use will depend on how many people you're addressing and how well you know them.

2) Here's when to use the informal 'you':

tú — for one person who's your friend, a family member or of a similar age.

vosotros/as — for a group of two or more people that you know.
Only use 'vosotras' if all the people in the group are female.

3) Use the formal 'you' for these people:

usted — for one person who is older than you or someone you don't know.

ustedes — for a group of two or more people that you don't know or who are older than you.

Section 2 — Pronouns

Direct Object Pronouns

Object pronouns replace the object of a sentence. In Spanish, there are two different types of object pronoun: direct and indirect.

Me, te, lo — me, you, him

Direct object pronouns are used when you're talking about who or what an action is done to (see p.7).

me	**me**	us	**nos**
you (informal singular)	**te**	you (informal plural)	**os**
him / it	**lo**	them (masculine)	**los**
her / it	**la**	them (feminine)	**las**
you (formal singular)	**lo/la**	you (formal plural)	**los/las**

Direct object pronouns usually go before the verb

1) You need to change the word order when using pronouns (see p.12-13 for more examples).
2) The pronoun usually goes before the verb.

Elena ve la película. → **Elena la ve.**
— Elena watches the film.   — Elena watches it.

The pronoun comes before the verb.

The action is done to the film (la película — feminine), so the pronoun 'it' needs to be in the feminine singular form.

Sofía saluda a mis amigos y a mí. → **Sofía nos saluda.**
— Sofía greets my friends and me.   — Sofía greets us.

Tomás lee el periódico. → **Tomás lo lee.**
— Tomás reads the newspaper.   — Tomás reads it.

Kristian huele las flores. → **Kristian las huele.**
— Kristian smells the flowers.   — Kristian smells them.

Section 2 — Pronouns

Indirect Object Pronouns

Me, te, les — to me, to you, to them

1) If you want to talk about doing something '<u>to</u>' ('a') or '<u>for</u>' ('para') <u>someone</u>, you need an <u>indirect object pronoun</u>.

to me	**me**	to us	**nos**
to you (informal singular)	**te**	to you (informal plural)	**os**
to him / her / it / you (formal singular)	**le**	to them / you (formal plural)	**les**

2) Like direct object pronouns, these pronouns also usually go <u>before</u> the <u>verb</u>:

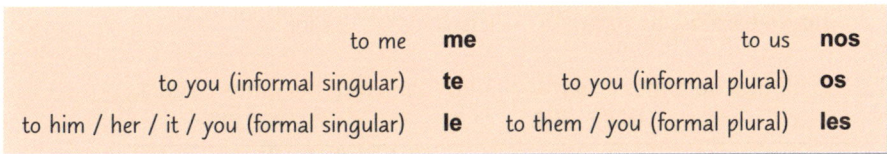

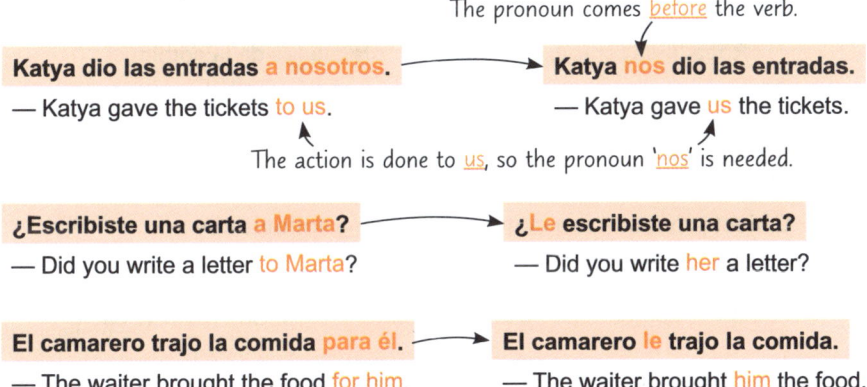

Indirect object pronouns with verbs like 'gustar'

1) <u>Indirect object pronouns</u> are the <u>same</u> ones you use with the verb '<u>gustar</u>'. This is because '<u>me</u> gusta el pan' literally means 'bread is pleasing <u>to me</u>'. The verbs '<u>encantar</u>', '<u>interesar</u>' and '<u>parecer</u>' also work in this way.

2) If what you like is <u>singular</u>, you need '<u>gusta</u>'. If it's <u>plural</u>, you need '<u>gustan</u>'.

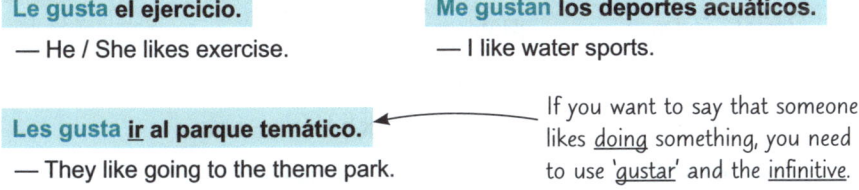

Section 2 — Pronouns

Ordering Pronouns

Some pronouns change after certain prepositions

1) The words for 'me' and 'you' (inf. sing.) become 'mí' and 'ti' after prepositions like 'a' (to), 'para' (for) and 'sobre' / 'de' (about).

   No es para mí, es para él. — It isn't for me, it's for him.

2) 'With me' becomes 'conmigo', and 'with you' becomes 'contigo'.

Object pronouns usually come before the verb

Direct and indirect object pronouns normally come before the verb in a sentence:

Rhea lo esperaba. — Rhea was waiting for it.

Jaime les da la comida. — Jaime gives them the food.

EXCEPTIONS

1) Object pronouns can come before a verb followed by an infinitive or be added to the end of an infinitive:

   La quiere comer. OR Quiere comerla. — He/She wants to eat it.

   You'd never say 'Quiere la comer'.

2) They can come before a phrase containing 'estar' and a present participle, or be added to the end of the present participle:

   Los estoy organizando. OR Estoy organizándolos. — I am organising them.

   You often need an accent to keep the pronunciation right.

Be careful with commands

1) When pronouns are used with positive commands, they are attached to the end of the verb:

   ¡Hazlo! — Do it!   **¡Háblame!** — Talk to me!

2) When pronouns are used with negative commands, they go between the negative word and the verb:

   ¡No lo comas! — Don't eat it!   **¡No me hagas reír!** — Don't make me laugh!

To form commands, you need to use the imperative (see p.72-73).

Section 2 — Pronouns

Combining direct and indirect object pronouns

When direct and indirect object pronouns are used in the same phrase, the indirect object pronoun comes first.

1	2	3
indirect object pronoun	direct object pronoun	verb

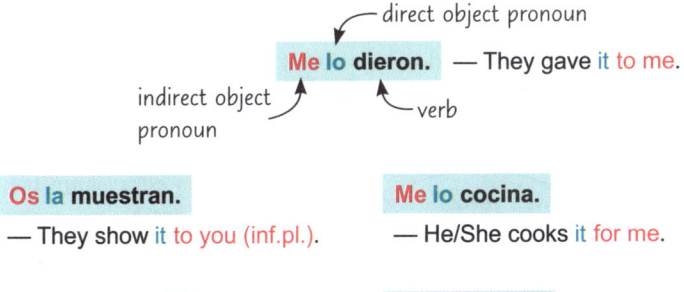

Me lo dieron. — They gave it to me.

Os la muestran.
— They show it to you (inf.pl.).

Me lo cocina.
— He/She cooks it for me.

Iván really wanted to push the boat out for dinner.

Nos lo describes.
— You describe him/it to us.

Te lo prepara.
— He/She prepares it for you.

'Se' can replace the indirect object pronoun

The indirect object pronouns 'le' and 'les' become 'se' in front of the direct object pronouns 'lo', 'la', 'los' or 'las'.

La doy a Rahul. ⟶ **Se la doy.**
— I give it to Rahul.   — I give it to him.

Los enviamos a ella. ⟶ **Se los enviamos.**
— We send them to her.   — We send them to her.

 When 'se' replaces the indirect object pronoun, you can add 'a él/ella', 'a usted', 'a ellos/ellas' or 'a ustedes' to make the meaning clear:
  Mi tío se lo explicó. ⟶ It isn't clear who he is explaining it to.
  Mi tío se lo explicó a ellos. — My uncle explained it to them.
You don't always need to add this though — it might be clear enough from the context or other sentences around it.

Section 2 — Pronouns

Relative Pronouns

'Who', 'which' and 'that' are relative pronouns

1) In English, relative pronouns are used to link two clauses or sentences together.

> He has a daughter. She is very tall. ⟶ He has a daughter **who** is very tall.
>
> — two sentences —
>
> The relative pronoun 'who' links the sentences together.

2) To talk about people, use 'who', and to talk about things, use 'that'. For animals, you can use 'which' if you're giving extra information about them, or 'that' if you're defining which ones they are.

> Maya saw a lizard, **which** was yellow.
> 'Which' is introducing extra information about this particular lizard.
>
> They stroked the dog **that** was in the garden.
> 'That' is used because there are lots of dogs, but they only stroked the one that was in the garden.

Use 'que' to add detail to a sentence

1) 'Que' can mean 'that', 'which' or 'who'.

2) You can use it to start a relative clause, which is a way of adding more information to a sentence.

> **Fui a un museo que se encuentra en el centro de la ciudad.**
> — I went to a museum that is situated in the city centre.

> **Hablé con la mujer que tiene la pastelería en la esquina.**
> — I spoke to the woman who owns the pastry shop on the corner.

> **La estación, que se llama Atocha, es muy grande.**
> — The station, which is called Atocha, is very big.

Relative pronouns can sometimes be missed out in English, but never in Spanish.

> The cat **(that)** we found was scared. ⟶ El gato **que** encontramos tenía miedo.

Section 2 — Pronouns

Use 'lo que' to talk about an idea

If you're talking about an idea instead of an object, you need to use 'lo que'.

Who, me?

> **Me echaron la culpa, lo que no era justo.**
> — They blamed me, which wasn't fair.

> **Come verduras con salsa de chocolate, lo que me parece raro.**
> — He eats vegetables with chocolate sauce, which seems strange to me.

Be careful after 'con', 'a' and 'de'

Use 'quien(es)' for people

Use 'quien' after prepositions like 'con', 'a' and 'de' to talk about people.

> **Me llevo bien con la chica a quien di el regalo.**
> — I get on well with the girl to whom I gave the present.

> **Confío en mis amigos, con quienes paso mucho tiempo.**
> — I trust my friends, with whom I spend lots of time.

If you're talking about more than one person, you need to use 'quienes'.

Use 'el/la que' or 'el/la cual' for 'that' and 'which'

After prepositions like 'con', 'a' and 'de', use 'el/la que' or 'el/la cual' for 'that' or 'which'.

> **Tengo una máquina con la que hago pan.**
> — I have a machine with which I make bread.

If the noun the sentence refers to is plural, use 'los/las que' or 'los/las cuales'.

> **Estos son las reglas a las cuales se refiere el profesor.**
> — These are the rules to which the teacher is referring.

de + el cual = del cual

> **Arreglé mi armario, por debajo del cual encontré mi camisa.**
> — I tidied my wardrobe, under which I found my shirt.

Section 2 — Pronouns

Interrogative Pronouns

Interrogative just means something that asks a question, so interrogative pronouns are just pronouns that are used to ask questions (see p.74 for more on questions).

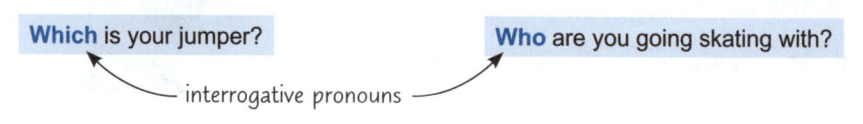

Which is your jumper?   **Who** are you going skating with?

— interrogative pronouns —

'¿Qué...' — 'What...'

'¿Qué...' is usually used when you'd use 'What...' in English.

¿Qué quieres cenar esta noche?
— **What** do you want for dinner tonight?

¿Qué vamos a hacer?
— **What** are we going to do?

'¿Cuál(es)...' — 'Which...' or 'Which one(s)...'

1) Use '¿Cuál(es)...' when you'd use 'Which...' or 'Which one(s)...' in English.

   ¿Cuál tiene la pantalla más grande?
   — **Which** (one) has the biggest screen?

   ¿Cuáles huelen mejor?
   — **Which** (ones) smell better?

   ¿Cuáles de las verduras no te gustan?
   — **Which** vegetables do you not like?

   Use 'cuáles' when you're asking about a plural thing.

2) '¿Cuál...' can also be used to say 'What...' in English. This is usually with the verb 'ser' to ask for a piece of information, rather than a definition.

   ¿Cuál es tu color preferido?
   — **What** is your favourite colour?

   ¿Cuál es tu número de teléfono?
   — **What** is your phone number?

'¿Quién(es)...' — 'Who...'

'¿Quién...' means 'Who...'. You often use it with prepositions.
'¿Quiénes...' is used when asking about more than one person.

¿Quién te llamó?
— **Who** called you?

¿Para quiénes son las entradas?
— **Who** are the tickets for?

Section 2 — Pronouns

Possessive Pronouns

Possessive pronouns must agree with the noun

1) Possessive pronouns show who something belongs to. They are used to say 'mine', 'yours', 'theirs' etc.

2) The pronoun must agree with the gender and number of the noun it replaces, not the person it belongs to.

3) That means that if you've got a noun that's feminine and singular, the pronoun that replaces it also needs to be feminine and singular.

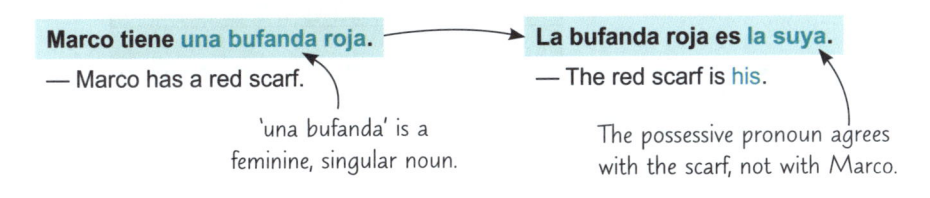

Marco tiene una bufanda roja.
— Marco has a red scarf.

'una bufanda' is a feminine, singular noun.

La bufanda roja es la suya.
— The red scarf is his.

The possessive pronoun agrees with the scarf, not with Marco.

Here are the possessive pronouns

	Singular		Plural	
	Masc.	Fem.	Masc.	Fem.
mine	el mío	la mía	los míos	las mías
yours (inf. sing.)	el tuyo	la tuya	los tuyos	las tuyas
his / hers / its / yours (form. sing.)	el suyo	la suya	los suyos	las suyas
ours	el nuestro	la nuestra	los nuestros	las nuestras
yours (inf. pl.)	el vuestro	la vuestra	los vuestros	las vuestras
theirs / yours (form. pl.)	el suyo	la suya	los suyos	las suyas

Here are some more examples of possessive pronouns in action:

¿Estos zapatos? Son los míos.
— These shoes? They're mine.

Don't forget that first person possessive pronouns need an accent, e.g. 'el mío', 'la mía'.

¿Has visto la tienda nueva en esta calle? Es la nuestra.
— Have you seen the new shop on this street? It's ours.

Section 2 — Pronouns

Demonstrative Pronouns

Use 'este', 'ese' and 'aquel' to talk about specific things

1) Demonstrative pronouns are used to specify exactly what you're talking about. They are the same as the demonstrative adjectives (see p.27).

2) Use 'este' to say 'this one', 'ese' to say 'that one' and 'aquel' to talk about something that's even further away, such as 'that one over there'.

3) Demonstrative pronouns must agree with the noun they refer back to:

	Singular		Plural	
	Masc.	Fem.	Masc.	Fem.
this / these one(s)	este	esta	estos	estas
that / those one(s)	ese	esa	esos	esas
that / those one(s) over there	aquel	aquella	aquellos	aquellas

La tienda tiene muchas camisetas. Compraré aquellas.
— The shop has lots of T-shirts. I will buy those ones (over there).

4) If the thing you're talking about doesn't have a clear or defined gender, or you're not mentioning it by name, use the neuter forms 'esto', 'eso' and 'aquello'.

¿Qué es esto?
— What's this?

Eso es falso.
— That's wrong.

'Algo' and 'alguien' — 'something' and 'someone'

'Algo' means 'something':

Necesito comer algo.
— I need to eat something.

'Algo' and 'alguien' are indefinite pronouns — they don't refer to a specific thing or person.

'Alguien' means 'someone':

Es alguien que me interesa.
— He/She is someone who interests me.

When you 'see someone' in Spanish, you have to add the personal 'a' (see p.81).

Vi a alguien que conozco en la panadería.
— I saw someone I know in the bakery.

Section 2 — Pronouns

Section 3 — Adjectives

The Essentials

Using Adjectives

Adjectives make sentences much more exciting.

1. Adjectives modify nouns

Adjectives tell you stuff about nouns by adding specific details.
They can tell you how something looks or feels.

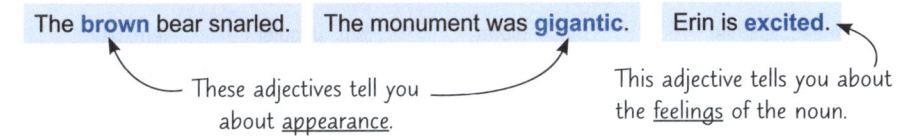

> The **brown** bear snarled. The monument was **gigantic**.   Erin is **excited**.
>
> ⎯ These adjectives tell you about appearance.   This adjective tells you about the feelings of the noun.

2. Some adjectives aren't obvious

It isn't always that obvious that some words are adjectives.

1) Words that show possession like 'my' and 'your' are possessive adjectives. Have a look at p.28 to find out more.

   > **His** house is orange. ⎯ The possessive adjective describes who the house belongs to.

2) Some adjectives, like 'this' and 'these', show that a noun is specific. These are demonstrative adjectives — see p.27.

   > **These** shoes are uncomfortable. ⎯ The demonstrative adjective here shows that they're not just any shoes, they're specific shoes.

3) Other adjectives help you form questions. These are interrogative adjectives, like 'Which..?' — see p.26.

   > **Which** dog stole my hotdog?
   >
   > **Which** train do we need to catch?

3. Use adjectives to say 'more...' or 'the most...'

Adjectives can be used as comparatives and superlatives (see p.30-31).

> Eduardo is **younger than** Edith.   ⎯ 'younger' is a comparative adjective.
>
> Pilar is the **fastest** runner on the team.   ⎯ 'fastest' is a superlative adjective.

Adjective Agreement

Spanish adjectives have to agree with the noun

1) In English, the adjective always stays the same: **fat** rat   **fat** rats

2) In Spanish, the adjective changes to match the noun. That means it changes depending on whether the noun is masculine, feminine, singular or plural (see p.3-4):

masc. singular	masc. plural	fem. singular	fem. plural
el hombre gord**o**	los hombres gord**os**	la rata gord**a**	las ratas gord**as**
— the fat man	— the fat men	— the fat rat	— the fat rats

'-o' changes to '-a' to make feminine adjectives

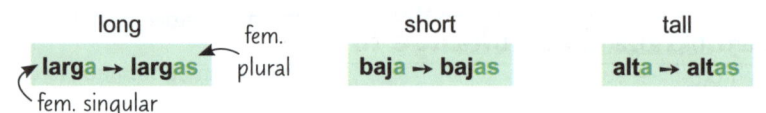

Adjectives ending in '-o' change the '-o' to '-a' in the feminine form.

masculine → **nuevo → nueva** ← feminine
— new

Add an '-s' to make plural adjectives

1) To make an adjective agree with a plural noun, you normally just add an '-s':

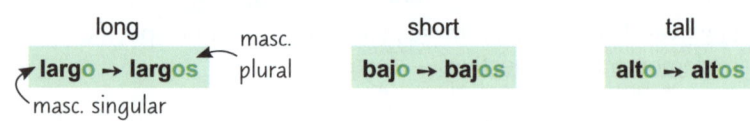

long — larg**o** → larg**os** (masc. singular / masc. plural)   short — baj**o** → baj**os**   tall — alt**o** → alt**os**

2) If it's a feminine plural noun, make the adjective feminine first, then add '-s':

long — larg**a** → larg**as** (fem. singular / fem. plural)   short — baj**a** → baj**as**   tall — alt**a** → alt**as**

Adjectives ending in '-or'

Adjectives ending in '-or', like 'trabajador' (hard-working), change to '-ora' in the feminine form. For the masculine plural, add '-es', and '-as' for the feminine plural.

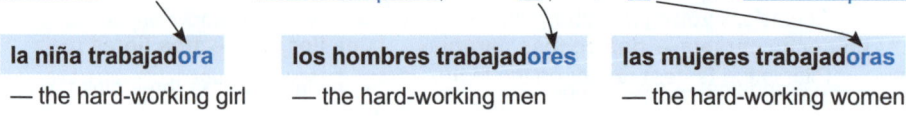

la niña trabajad**ora**	los hombres trabajad**ores**	las mujeres trabajad**oras**
— the hard-working girl	— the hard-working men	— the hard-working women

Section 3 — Adjectives

Some adjectives only change in the plural

Adjectives ending in '-e' or a consonant

Adjectives which don't end in '-o' don't change in the singular. If the noun is plural, add '-s' if it ends in a vowel and '-es' if it ends in a consonant.

el perro grande — the big dog
los perros grandes — the big dogs

la tarea difícil — the difficult task
las tareas difíciles — the difficult tasks

'-z' changes to '-ces' in the plural

If an adjective ends in '-z' in the singular, remove the '-z' and add '-ces' in the plural:

la chica feliz → las chicas felices
— the happy girl — the happy girls

See p.4 for nouns that work in a similar way.

Adjectives ending in '-ista'

To make an adjective ending in '-ista' plural, just add an '-s'. It's the same for masculine and feminine nouns.

masc. / fem. singular   masc. / fem. plural
           optim**ista** → optim**istas**
                — optimistic

Some adjectives don't change to agree

There are some adjectives (mostly colours) which don't change at all, regardless of gender and number.

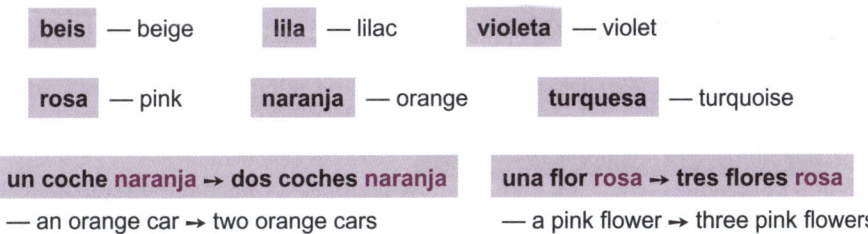

beis — beige
rosa — pink

lila — lilac
naranja — orange

violeta — violet
turquesa — turquoise

un coche naranja → dos coches naranja
— an orange car → two orange cars

una flor rosa → tres flores rosa
— a pink flower → three pink flowers

Section 3 — Adjectives

Adjective Position

Most adjectives go after the noun

1) In English, adjectives usually go before the noun they're describing:

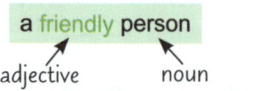
a friendly person
adjective   noun

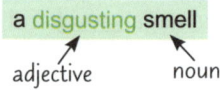
a disgusting smell
adjective   noun

2) In Spanish, the adjective normally goes after the noun:

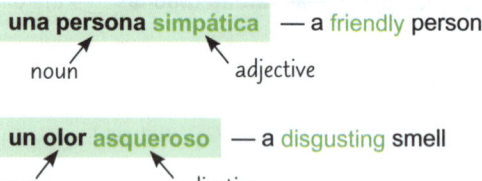

una persona simpática — a friendly person
noun   adjective

un olor asqueroso — a disgusting smell
noun   adjective

All Tiberio could smell was his next meal.

Some adjectives go in front of the noun

1) In Spanish, some adjectives always go in front of the noun they're describing.
2) They agree in gender and number.

mucho/a	a lot of
muchos/as	lots of
poco/a	little
pocos/as	few

tanto/a	so much
tantos/as	so many
otro/a	another
otros/as	other

próximo/a	next
último/a	last
alguno/a	some
cada	each

Había muchos turistas en la plaza.
— There were lots of tourists in the square.

Las últimas celebraciones tuvieron lugar en agosto.
— The last celebrations took place in August.

'Otro/a/os/as', 'cada' and 'alguno/a' are all indefinite adjectives (see p.25).

3) Ordinal numbers work in the same way:

primero/a, segundo/a, tercero/a...   first, second, third...

Han perdido la segunda pelota. — They have lost the second ball.

Section 3 — Adjectives

Some adjectives change before masculine nouns

Some adjectives drop a letter

Some adjectives <u>lose</u> the final '-<u>o</u>' when they go in front of a <u>masculine singular noun</u>.

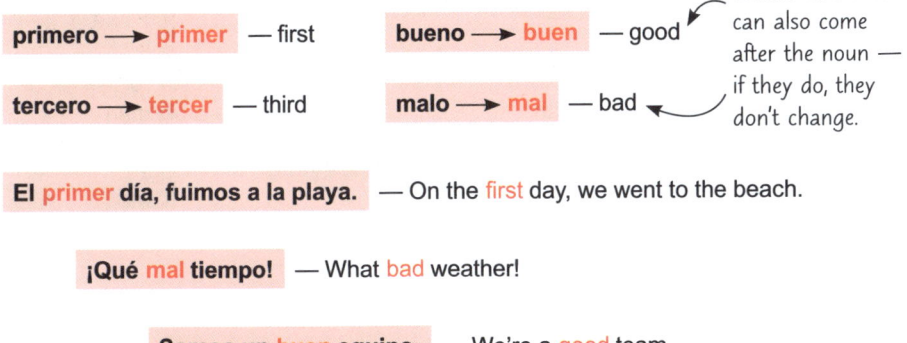

'Bueno' and 'malo' can also come after the noun — if they do, they don't change.

primero → primer — first
tercero → tercer — third
bueno → buen — good
malo → mal — bad

El primer día, fuimos a la playa. — On the first day, we went to the beach.

¡Qué mal tiempo! — What bad weather!

Somos un buen equipo. — We're a good team.

Some adjectives drop a letter and add an accent

The adjectives '<u>alguno/a</u>' and '<u>ninguno/a</u>' <u>drop</u> the final '-<u>o</u>' and <u>add</u> an <u>accent</u> when they go before <u>masculine singular</u> nouns.

Algún día te explicaré todo. — Some day I'll explain everything to you.

No queda ningún pimiento verde. — There is no green pepper left.

'Grande' becomes 'gran' before singular nouns

'<u>Grande</u>' is the only adjective that <u>drops</u> '-<u>de</u>' in front of both <u>masculine and feminine</u> singular nouns.

'Grande' can go before or after a noun. Its meaning changes depending on its position (see p.24).

Miguel es un gran hombre. — Miguel is a great man.

Es una gran manera de conocer a otra gente.
— It's a great way to meet other people.

Section 3 — Adjectives

Adjective Position

Position can change an adjective's meaning

The meaning of certain adjectives changes depending on whether they come before the noun or after it. These are some of the most important ones:

'grande' — 'great' or 'big'

Before the noun: **un gran hombre**   After the noun: **un hombre grande**
— a great man   — a big man

In context: **Cada gran hombre tiene un caballo grande.**
— Every great man has a big horse.

'mismo' — 'same' or 'myself'

Before the noun: **el mismo día**   After the noun: **yo mismo**
— the same day   — I myself

In context: **Lo encontré yo mismo ese mismo día.**
— I found it myself that same day.

'nuevo' — 'new (to owner)' or 'brand new'

Before the noun: **un nuevo coche**   After the noun: **un coche nuevo**
— a new (to owner) car   — a brand new car

In context: **Él tiene un nuevo coche, pero ella tiene un coche nuevo.**
— He has a new car, but she has a brand new car.

'viejo' — 'old (long-standing)' or 'old (elderly)'

Before the noun: **un viejo amigo**   After the noun: **un amigo viejo**
— an old (long-standing) friend   — an old (elderly) friend

In context: **Tengo muchos viejos amigos, pero no tengo amigos viejos.**
— I have lots of long-standing friends, but I don't have any elderly friends.

Section 3 — Adjectives

Indefinite Adjectives

1) Indefinite adjectives are words like 'another', 'all', 'some', 'each' and 'any'. They give more information about the noun.

2) Indefinite adjectives go before the noun.

> It rained all night.
> indefinite adjective → ← noun

> He inspected each item carefully.
> indefinite adjective → ← noun

3) In Spanish, most indefinite adjectives agree with the noun they describe.

'Another', 'all', 'some', 'each' and 'any'

1) 'Otro' and 'otra' mean 'another'. Their plural forms, 'otros' and 'otras', mean 'other'.

> Compraré otro bolso. — I will buy another bag.

2) 'Todo/a/os/as' means 'all'.

> El perro destruyó todos mis zapatos.
> — The dog destroyed all my shoes.

Thank goodness he didn't get his paws on my favourite top...

3) Use 'algún', 'alguna' or 'algunos/as' to mean 'some'.

> Algunas cebollas tienen un olor fuerte. — Some onions have a strong smell.

4) 'Cada' means 'each'. It's always used with singular nouns and it doesn't change for masculine and feminine nouns.

> La veo cada semana. — I see her each week.

EXCEPTIONS

There's no special word for 'any' in Spanish.

> ¿Hay leche en la nevera? — Is there any milk in the fridge?
>
> ↖ You could also translate this as 'Is there milk in the fridge?'

Section 3 — Adjectives

Interrogative Adjectives

'¿Qué...' — 'What...'

1) When you want to ask a question using 'What...', you can use the interrogative adjective '¿Qué...'.

   Interrogative adjectives are always written with an accent.

2) '¿Qué...' means 'What...' and is used to refer to things or ideas:

   ¿Qué tipo es?
   — What type is it?

   ¿Qué libros preferís?
   — What books do you prefer?

3) '¿Qué...' never changes to agree with a noun it's describing.

   ¿Qué deportes juegan?
   — What sports do they play?

   ¿Qué asignaturas estudias?
   — What subjects do you study?

'¿Cuánto...' means 'How much...' or 'How many...'

1) If you want to ask how much of something there is or how many of something there are, you'll need to use '¿Cuánto...'.

2) '¿Cuánto...' needs to agree in gender and number with the noun that follows:

   See p.74 for more on asking questions.

   ¿Cuánto tiempo queda?
   — How much time is left?

   ¿Cuánta leche bebes al día?
   — How much milk do you drink a day?

   ¿Cuántos libros hay?
   — How many books are there?

   ¿Cuántas personas están aquí?
   — How many people are here?

The girls hadn't realised the self timer wasn't on.

Section 3 — Adjectives

Demonstrative Adjectives

'Este' and 'estos' — 'this' and 'these'

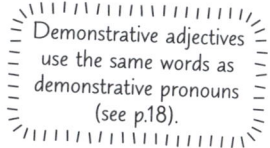
Demonstrative adjectives use the same words as demonstrative pronouns (see p.18).

1) To say 'this' in Spanish, use the adjective 'este'. It has to agree with the noun, so use 'esta' if it's feminine.

   Me gusta este libro.
   — I like this book.

   Nunca he visto esta película.
   — I have never seen this film.

2) To say 'these', use 'estos' for masculine nouns and 'estas' for feminine nouns.

   Prefiero estos plátanos.
   — I prefer these bananas.

   Me dieron estas camisas.
   — They gave me these shirts.

'Ese' and 'aquel' — 'that' and 'that (over there)'

1) There are two ways to say 'that' in Spanish, but their meanings are slightly different.

2) 'Ese' is used when you'd normally say 'that' in English. Use 'esa' for feminine nouns and 'esos' (masculine) or 'esas' (feminine) for plurals.

   Vive en ese bosque.
   — He / She lives in that forest.

   Quisiera comprar esa mochila.
   — I would like to buy that rucksack.

   Dibujaron esos árboles.
   — They drew those trees.

   Hago un pastel con esas peras.
   — I'm making a cake with those pears.

3) If you want to say 'that over there', you need to use 'aquel'. 'Aquel' changes to 'aquella' in the feminine form and 'aquellos' and 'aquellas' in the plural forms.

   aquel tigre
   — that tiger over there

   aquellas flores
   — those flowers over there

   aquella montaña
   — that mountain over there

   aquellos gauchos
   — those cowboys over there

Section 3 — Adjectives

Possessive and Relative Adjectives

Possessive adjectives show you who or what owns something.

Your brother is rude.   Today is my birthday.

Learn all the possessive adjectives

1) In Spanish, words like 'my' and 'your' agree with the noun they're describing — not the owner.
2) The possessive adjectives go before the noun to show who owns it.

	Singular		Plural	
	Masc.	Fem.	Masc.	Fem.
my	mi	mi	mis	mis
your (inf. sing.)	tu	tu	tus	tus
his / her / its / your (form. sing.)	su	su	sus	sus
our	nuestro	nuestra	nuestros	nuestras
your (inf. pl.)	vuestro	vuestra	vuestros	vuestras
their / your (form. pl.)	su	su	sus	sus

Tu conejo tiene orejas muy grandes. — Your rabbit has very big ears.

'Conejo' is a singular noun, so 'tu' needs to be in the singular as well.

Nuestros vecinos son simpáticos. — Our neighbours are friendly.

'Vecinos' is a masculine plural noun, so the possessive adjective must be masculine plural too.

'Su(s)' can mean 'his', 'her', 'its', 'their' and 'your' (formal). Use the rest of the information in the sentence to work out which of these it is.

Jorge todavía no ha limpiado sus botas.   In this sentence, the subject of the verb is Jorge
(Jorge still hasn't cleaned his boots.)   — so the word 'sus' is likely to mean 'his'.

Section 3 — Adjectives

Possessive adjectives have different forms

1) There are also long forms of possessive adjectives in Spanish — these ones go after the noun and put the emphasis on the adjective instead of the noun.
2) These long forms agree with the noun in the same way as the short forms.

| | Singular || Plural ||
	Masc.	Fem.	Masc.	Fem.
my	mío	mía	míos	mías
your (inf. sing.)	tuyo	tuya	tuyos	tuyas
his / her / its / your (form. sing.)	suyo	suya	suyos	suyas
our	nuestro	nuestra	nuestros	nuestras
your (inf. pl.)	vuestro	vuestra	vuestros	vuestras
their / your (form. pl.)	suyo	suya	suyos	suyas

Sona es una amiga mía. — Sona is my friend.

'Mía' agrees with 'una amiga', which is a feminine noun.

La tortuga tuya se mueve lentamente. — Your tortoise moves slowly.

'Cuyo' — whose

1) 'Cuyo' is a relative adjective. Use it when you want to say 'whose' in Spanish to show who something belongs to.
2) The ending of 'cuyo' agrees with the noun that follows it, not with its owner.

Este es el hombre cuyo niño llora.
— This is the man whose child cries.

'Cuyo' agrees with 'niño', which is a masculine singular noun.

Aquí está el hombre cuyas gafas son azules.
— Here's the man whose glasses are blue.

'Cuyas' agrees with 'gafas', which is a feminine plural noun.

Section 3 — Adjectives

Comparative Adjectives

1) Comparative adjectives let you compare things.
2) Comparative adjectives in English are made by adding '-er' to the end of a short adjective, or by putting 'more' or 'less' in front of longer adjectives.

> Yonas is louder than Kim.
> Yonas is more polite than Kim.
> — comparative adjective —

3) You can use 'as... as' to say something is the same as something else.

'More... than', 'less... than', 'as... as'

1) In Spanish, you can't say 'cheaper (than)', you have to say 'more cheap (than)' — use 'más... (que)'.

> Ese bocadillo es más barato (que ese).
> — That sandwich is cheaper (than that one).

"Who are you calling cheap?"

2) If you want to say something is 'less cheap (than)', use 'menos... (que)'.

> Ese bocadillo es menos barato (que ese).
> — That sandwich is less cheap (than that one).

3) To say something is 'as cheap as' something else, use 'tan... como'.

> Este bocadillo es tan barato como ese bocadillo.
> — This sandwich is as cheap as that sandwich.

EXCEPTIONS

Some comparatives are formed differently. You'll have to learn what they are.

Adjective	Comparative
bueno (good)	mejor (better)
malo (bad)	peor (worse)
viejo (old)	mayor (older — for people only)
joven (young)	menor (younger — for people only)

These comparatives stay the same for the masculine and feminine forms, but they add '-es' for the plural forms.

> Esta telenovela es mejor.
> — This soap opera is better.

> Mis hermanas son mayores que yo.
> — My sisters are older than me.

Section 3 — Adjectives

Superlative Adjectives

Superlative adjectives are for saying something is 'the most / least something'. In English you add '-est' to the end of a short adjective or put 'the most / least' in front of longer adjectives:

> Timon is the loudest.   Yanika is the most polite.
> ⎣ superlative adjective ⎦

Describe something as 'the most' or 'the least'

1) To say something is 'the most' something in Spanish, use 'el más'.

   > Este coche es práctico. → Este coche es el más práctico.
   > — This car is practical.   — This car is the most practical.

2) To say something is 'the least' something, use 'el menos'.

   > Los tres coches son prácticos, pero este coche es el menos práctico.
   > — All three cars are practical, but this car is the least practical.

3) If the noun is feminine, you'll need to change the 'el' to 'la', and if it's plural, change it to 'los' or 'las'.

   > Estos zapatos son los más prácticos.   — These shoes are the most practical.

EXCEPTIONS

There are some irregular superlative adjectives.

Adjective	Superlative
bueno (good)	el mejor (the best)
malo (bad)	el peor (the worst)
viejo (old)	el mayor (the oldest — for people only)
joven (young)	el menor (the youngest — for people only)

If these refer to a feminine noun, use 'la'. If they refer to a plural noun, add '-es' to their endings and use 'los' or 'las'.

> Esta tortilla es la peor.   Estos son los hermanos menores de Juan.
> — This omelette is the worst.   — These are Juan's youngest siblings.

Section 3 — Adjectives

Section 4 — Adverbs

Using Adverbs

The Essentials

Adverbs describe verbs by adding more information about how an action is done. Using them makes your Spanish much more interesting and complex.

1. Adverbs describe verbs

1) Adverbs tell you how or when an action happens. Most adverbs in English end in '-ly'. See p.33 for how regular Spanish adverbs work.

> The child spoke quietly.

The adverb describes the verb — it tells you that the speaking was done quietly.

2) Adverbs don't always just have to be a single word. They can be a phrase — an adverbial phrase. See p.35 for more on these in Spanish.

> The child spoke as quietly as a mouse.

The whole phrase tells you how the child spoke.

3) Quantifiers are a type of adverb — they tell you how much of something there is. See p.36.

> I have too many hats.

Quantifiers give you an idea of how many things there are.

> He has enough cheese.

4) Some adverbs describe adjectives. Adverbs like 'very' and 'quite' are called intensifiers — see p.36.

> The restaurant was quite busy.

The adverb describes how busy the restaurant was.

2. Don't confuse adjectives and adverbs

To check if it's an adjective or an adverb, see if it's describing the noun or not:

> I had a late lunch.

'Late' is an adjective because it describes the noun 'lunch'.

> I left the house late.

'Late' is an adverb in this sentence. It describes the verb 'left'.

3. Use adverbs to say 'more...' or 'the most...'

Adverbs can be used to form comparatives and superlatives (see p.37).

> I laugh more loudly than you.

comparative adverb

> I laugh the most loudly.

superlative adverb

Useful Adverbs

Adverbs say how someone does something

1) In English, you don't say 'I walk quick' — you have to add '-ly' to the end of the adjective to say 'I walk quickly'.
2) In Spanish, you add '-mente' to the end of the adjective to form an adverb. You need to make sure the adjective is in the feminine form first.

ADVERB = FEMININE ADJECTIVE + '-MENTE'

Camino rápidamente. — I walk quickly.

The word for 'quick' is 'rápido', and the feminine version is 'rápida'. Add '-mente' to get 'rápidamente' (quickly).

3) With adjectives that don't end in '-o', you can just add '-mente':

triste (sad) → tristemente (sadly)
fácil (easy) → fácilmente (easily)

4) Adverbs come after the verb and they don't need to agree. This is because they're describing an action, not the person doing the action.

Mi tío habla lentamente. — My uncle speaks slowly.

EXCEPTIONS

Not every adverb follows the rules — these are some irregulars.

adjective	adverb
bueno/a	bien
malo/a	mal

Nadamos bien. — We swim well.

Nadamos mal. — We swim badly.

You can also form adverbs with 'con'

1) In English, you can say someone did something 'with patience' instead of saying 'patiently'.
2) You can do the same in Spanish by putting 'con' with a noun.

Les esperé con paciencia. — I waited for them patiently / with patience.

Section 4 — Adverbs

Other Useful Adverbs

Some adverbs are used to form questions

Interrogative adverbs are used in questions and are always written with an accent.

¿Cómo...	How...
¿Cuándo...	When...
¿Dónde...	Where...
¿Por qué...	Why...
¿Cuánto...	How much...

¿Cuándo visitarán a sus abuelos?
— When will they visit their grandparents?

¿Dónde dejaste las llaves?
— Where did you leave the keys?

When used as an adverb, '¿Cuánto...' doesn't change to agree.

¿Cuánto cuesta un kilo de arroz?
— How much does one kilo of rice cost?

Adverbs can give you details about time...

Adverbs of time tell you when or how often something happens. Most go after the verb, but it's more common to put 'todavía' and 'ya' before the verb.

después (de)	after
antes (de)	before
pronto	soon

ahora	now
todavía	still
ya	already

Tendrá que irse pronto.
— He / She will have to leave soon.

Ya tengo dinero suficiente.
— I already have enough money.

...or place

Adverbs of place explain where something happens.

aquí	here
ahí	(just) there
allá / allí	(over) there
cerca	near
lejos	far away

Están allí, cerca del castillo.
— They're over there, near the castle.

El lago está lejos, pero el río está ahí.
— The lake is far away, but the river is just here.

Section 4 — Adverbs

Adverbial Phrases

Adverbial phrases help you give more info

1) An adverbial phrase is a group of words that does the same job as a single-word adverb:

   He walks to work as often as possible.

   'As often as possible' is an adverbial phrase because it describes the verb 'walks'.

2) It's the same thing in Spanish — an adverbial phrase can give you more information about the verb.

   Saib nunca anda. Corre todo el tiempo.
   — Saib never walks. He runs all the time.

   'Todo el tiempo' describes the verb 'corre'.

   Todos hablaban al mismo tiempo.
   — Everyone was talking at the same time.

   'Al mismo tiempo' describes the verb 'hablaban'.

Use Spanish adverbial phrases to add more detail

Every now and then, try to get an adverbial phrase into your work. It'll make your Spanish sound more impressive.

Here are some more examples:

por todas partes	— everywhere	**mientras tanto**	— meanwhile
al mismo tiempo	— at the same time	**a diario**	— daily
de momento	— at the moment	**a menudo**	— often
de repente	— suddenly	**a veces**	— sometimes
de nuevo	— again	**de vez en cuando**	— from time to time
en seguida	— straightaway	**pocas veces**	— rarely, seldom

Pocas veces escucho música clásica. — I rarely listen to classical music.

Contestó al teléfono en seguida. — He / She answered the phone straightaway.

Section 4 — Adverbs

Quantifiers and Intensifiers

Use quantifiers to say 'how many' or 'how much'

1) Quantifiers are adverbs that usually go before the noun to describe how many or how much of something there is:

mucho	a lot / lots of
poco	only a little / only a few
un poco de	a bit of

demasiado	too much / too many
tanto	so much / so many
bastante	enough

Hubo muchas tormentas el mes pasado.
— There were lots of storms last month.

When used with nouns, quantifiers have to agree with what they're describing.

2) You can also use quantifiers with verbs — they go after the verb and don't change their endings.

Talia trabaja demasiado.
— Talia works too much.

'Demasiado' is describing the verb, so it doesn't change.

Use intensifiers to strengthen what you're saying

1) You can use intensifiers like 'very' and 'quite' to add detail to what you're saying.

2) Intensifiers go before the word they modify, but their endings don't change.

muy	very
poco	not very

demasiado	too
bastante	quite

Estoy muy enfadada contigo.
— I'm very angry with you.

Esta película es demasiado violenta.
— This film is too violent.

3) You can add 'ito/a/os/as' to the end of most adjectives to make something seem smaller or cuter.

El bebé está enfermito.
— The baby is poorly.

4) Add 'ísimo/a/os/as' to make the meaning of what you're saying stronger.

Carla es altísima.
— Carla is really tall.

Section 4 — Adverbs

Comparative and Superlative Adverbs

Compare how something is done

1) Comparative adverbs let you compare how something is done. In English, this is usually done by adding 'more' or 'less' in front of the adverb.

   Jaione works **less slowly** than me.

2) And it works exactly the same in Spanish:

   Jaione trabaja más lentamente que yo.
   — Jaione works more slowly than me.

   Jaione trabaja menos lentamente que yo.
   — Jaione works less slowly than me.

   'Más' (more) or 'menos' (less) go before the adverb and 'que' (than) goes after it.

3) If you want to say someone does something 'as... as' someone else, use 'tan... como'.

   Jaione trabaja tan lentamente como yo.
   — Jaione works as slowly as me.

Say something is 'the most' or 'the least'

For superlative adverbs, you need to follow this pattern:

Pedro es el que canta más tranquilamente.
— Pedro sings the quietest.
(This literally translates as 'Pedro is the one who sings most quietly.')

'El' changes to 'la/los/las', depending on the subject.

EXCEPTIONS

There are some comparative and superlative adverbs that just have to be learnt:

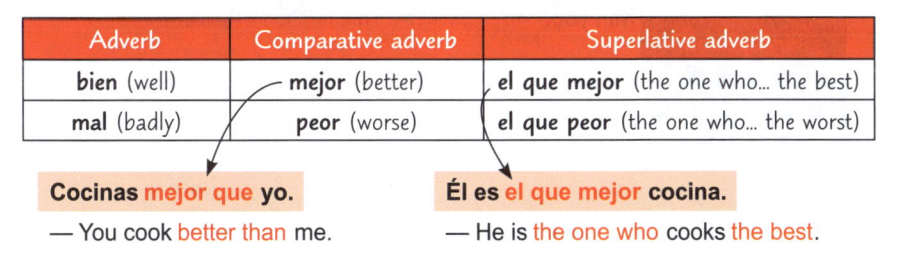

Adverb	Comparative adverb	Superlative adverb
bien (well)	mejor (better)	el que mejor (the one who... the best)
mal (badly)	peor (worse)	el que peor (the one who... the worst)

Cocinas mejor que yo.
— You cook better than me.

Él es el que mejor cocina.
— He is the one who cooks the best.

Section 4 — Adverbs

Section 5 — Verbs

The Essentials — **Using Verbs**

The next few pages are a reminder of some verb basics. There's not a lot you can do without verbs so make sure you know what they are and how to use them.

1. Verbs are doing or being words

1) A verb is an action word — a 'doing' or 'being' word.

2) Doing words describe actions: | Verónica **throws** the frisbee.

3) Most being words come from the verb 'to be': | Luca **is** a quick runner.

4) In Spanish, there are two verbs that mean 'to be' — 'ser' and 'estar' (see p.46-47).

2. All parts of the verb come from the infinitive

1) The infinitive is the form of the verb that you find in the dictionary.

   'echar' — to throw   'ser' — to be

2) To use a verb, you need to know its infinitive (see p.41).

3) The infinitive tells you what's happening, but NOT who's doing the action or when. You have to change it so it's right for the person and time you're talking about.

3. The subject pronoun tells you who does something

The person (or thing) doing the verb is the subject of the sentence. These are the subject pronouns in English:

	Singular	Plural
First person	I	we
Second person	you	you
Third person	he / she / it	they

Subject pronouns aren't used very often in Spanish though (see p.8) — you can tell who's doing the verb by the verb ending.

Section 5 — Verbs

4. The verb agrees with its subject

The verb changes to agree with its subject. This is called conjugation.
The way it changes depends on the tense.
This is how the verb 'to be' is conjugated in the present tense in English:

I am	we are
you are	you are
he/she/it is	they are

5. The tense tells you when something happens

Verbs can be put into different tenses to tell you when things happen.

Tenses in the Past	When is it used?	Example:
Preterite (p.52-53)	When something happened suddenly, or has been completed.	Kai baked a pie.
Imperfect (p.54-55)	When something went on for a while.	Kai was baking a pie. Kai used to bake pies.
Perfect (p.56)	When something has happened recently.	Kai has baked a pie.
Pluperfect (p.58)	When something happened before something else in the past.	Kai had baked a pie.

Tenses in the Present	When is it used?	Example:
Present (p.42-43)	When something is happening now, or happens repeatedly.	Kai bakes a pie. Kai bakes pies.
Present Continuous (p.63)	When something is happening right now.	Kai is baking a pie.

Tenses in the Future	When is it used?	Example:
Immediate Future (p.59)	When something is going to happen.	Kai is going to bake a pie.
Proper Future (p.60)	When something will happen at some point in the future.	Kai will bake a pie.
Conditional (p.61)	When something could happen, but might not.	Kai would bake a pie, if...

Section 5 — Verbs

6. The mood tells you the speaker's feelings

1) Mood tells you how the speaker feels towards a verb, for example, whether it's likely to happen or if it's a command. Here are some moods you should know:

Mood	When is it used?	Example:
Imperative (p.72-73)	When you want to give someone an order or make a request.	Bake a pie, Kai!
Present Subjunctive (p.68-70)	When there's doubt or you want to express a wish or desire.	I hope Kai bakes a cake.

2) The imperfect subjunctive is also a mood in Spanish (see p.71). It is used in the same situations as the present subjunctive, but talks about actions in the past. You only need to be able to recognise it — you don't need to be able to use it.

3) There is one expression in the imperfect subjunctive that you do need to be able to use though — 'quisiera' (I would like). See p.71.

7. Sentences can be active or passive

1) In an active sentence, the subject does the action described by the verb.

The goat eats the carrots.
subject → ← object

2) In a passive sentence, the object becomes the subject, and something is done to the subject.

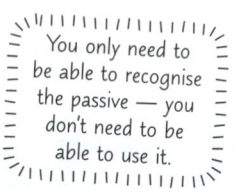

The carrots are eaten by the goat.
subject →

You only need to be able to recognise the passive — you don't need to be able to use it.

3) Passive sentences have different tenses, just as active sentences do (see p.66).

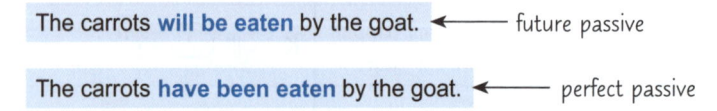

The carrots **will be eaten** by the goat. ← future passive

The carrots **have been eaten** by the goat. ← perfect passive

Section 5 — Verbs

Infinitives

You'll see the infinitive a lot, so make sure you've got your head around it.

Verbs in the dictionary are in the infinitive

1) When you look up a verb in the dictionary, it will be in its infinitive form.
2) In Spanish, this is the form that ends with '-ar', '-er' and '-ir' (see p.42).

   Spanish infinitive → **record**ar → (to remember) ← English infinitive

3) The English infinitive is formed by putting 'to' in front of the verb.
4) Often, you need to conjugate the verb before you can use it (see p.39).
5) Sometimes though, you have to use the verb in its infinitive form.

The infinitive often follows another verb

1) When you use two verbs together, the second is usually in the infinitive.
2) To say 'I want to play basketball', you need to use two verbs.
3) The first verb, 'to want to' ('querer'), is conjugated to match the subject.
4) The second verb, 'to play' ('jugar'), is in the infinitive.

   Quiero jugar al baloncesto. — I want to play basketball.
   conjugated verb   infinitive

Other useful ways of using the infinitive

1) The infinitive can be used as a noun and act as the subject of a sentence.

   Escuchar música me hace feliz. — Listening to music makes me happy.

2) It is often used after prepositions such as 'de' and 'para'.

   Me alegro de ver a tu hermana. — I'm happy to see your sister.

   Para llegar a la estación, siga todo recto. — To get to the station, go straight on.

Present Tense — Regular Verbs

The present tense tells you what is happening

1) Use the present tense for actions that are happening now or that happen regularly.

   Me cambio la ropa. — I change my clothes / I am changing my clothes.

2) You can also use the present tense for things that are about to happen.

   Hoy vamos a las Islas Canarias.
   — Today we are going to the Canary Islands.

   It didn't feel like a day over nine years and 364 days.

3) Use the present tense with 'desde hace' to say how long you've been doing something or how long you've known someone.

   Practico la natación desde hace diez años.
   — I have been swimming for ten years.

   Nos conocemos desde hace mucho tiempo.
   — We have known each other for a long time.

Present tense verbs are made of stems + endings

1) Regular verbs follow set patterns when they change to match the subject of a sentence. In Spanish, most regular verbs end in '-ar', '-er' or '-ir'.

2) To form the present tense of these regular verbs, you need to find the stem. To do this, remove the last two letters from the infinitive.

	'-ar' verbs	'-er' verbs	'-ir' verbs
Infinitive	hablar	comer	vivir
Stem	habl-	com-	viv-

3) Next, you have to put an ending on the stem. The ending shows who's doing the action and is different for each type of verb.

Present Tense — Verb Endings

You need to add <u>different endings</u> to different <u>types of verb</u> — as long as you know these endings, you can form the <u>present tense</u> of <u>any regular verb</u>.

'-ar' verb endings

For '-<u>ar</u>' verbs like '<u>hablar</u>' (to speak), these are the <u>endings</u> you need to add:

I speak	**hablo**	**hablamos**	we speak
you (inf. sing.) speak	**hablas**	**habláis**	you (inf. pl.) speak
he/she/it/you (form. sing.) speak(s)	**habla**	**hablan**	they/you (form. pl.) speak

<u>Other verbs</u> that follow this pattern include '<u>pasar</u>' (to happen / to spend time), '<u>llevar</u>' (to take) and '<u>esperar</u>' (to wait for / to hope).

'-er' verb endings

For '-<u>er</u>' verbs like '<u>comer</u>' (to eat), here are the <u>endings</u> to add to the stem:

I eat	**como**	**comemos**	we eat
you (inf. sing.) eat	**comes**	**coméis**	you (inf. pl.) eat
he/she/it/you (form. sing.) eat(s)	**come**	**comen**	they/you (form. pl.) eat

There are <u>other verbs</u> that follow this pattern, including '<u>correr</u>' (to run), '<u>vender</u>' (to sell) and '<u>comprender</u>' (to understand).

'-ir' verb endings

For '-<u>ir</u>' verbs like '<u>vivir</u>' (to live), add these <u>endings</u> to the stem:

I live	**vivo**	**vivimos**	we live
you (inf. sing.) live	**vives**	**vivís**	you (inf. pl.) live
he/she/it/you (form. sing.) live(s)	**vive**	**viven**	they/you (form. pl.) live

<u>Other verbs</u> that behave like this include '<u>recibir</u>' (to receive), '<u>subir</u>' (to go up) and '<u>permitir</u>' (to allow).

Section 5 — Verbs

Radical-Changing Verbs

Radical-changing verbs change their stems

1) Radical-changing (or 'stem-changing') verbs are ones that change their spelling in certain conjugations.

2) In the present tense, their stems change in every form apart from the 'we' and 'you (inf. pl.)' forms.

3) Even though their stems change, their endings stay regular.

I don't know how else to say it, Vern — you've changed...

e → ie, e.g. 'pensar' (to think)

I think	p**ie**nso	pensamos	we think
you (inf. sing.) think	p**ie**nsas	pensáis	you (inf. pl.) think
he/she/it/you (form. sing.) think(s)	p**ie**nsa	p**ie**nsan	they/you (form. pl.) think

Other verbs that follow this pattern: **venir** — to come   **tener** — to have

'Tener' and 'venir' have irregular first person singular forms — 'tengo' and 'vengo'.

o / u → ue, e.g. 'poder' (to be able to)

I can	p**ue**do	podemos	we can
you (inf. sing.) can	p**ue**des	podéis	you (inf. pl.) can
he/she/it/you (form. sing.) can	p**ue**de	p**ue**den	they/you (form. pl.) can

Other verbs that follow this pattern: **j**u**gar** — to play   **d**o**rmir** — to sleep

e → i, e.g. 'pedir' (to ask for)

This change only happens in '-ir' verbs.

I ask for	p**i**do	pedimos	we ask for
you (inf. sing.) ask for	p**i**des	pedís	you (inf. pl.) ask for
he/she/it/you (form. sing.) ask(s) for	p**i**de	p**i**den	they/you (form. pl.) ask for

Other verbs that follow this pattern: **ve**stirse — to get dressed   **re**ír — to laugh

Section 5 — Verbs

Irregular Verbs

In Spanish, the verbs 'to go', 'to give', 'to do / to make' and 'to know' are irregular.

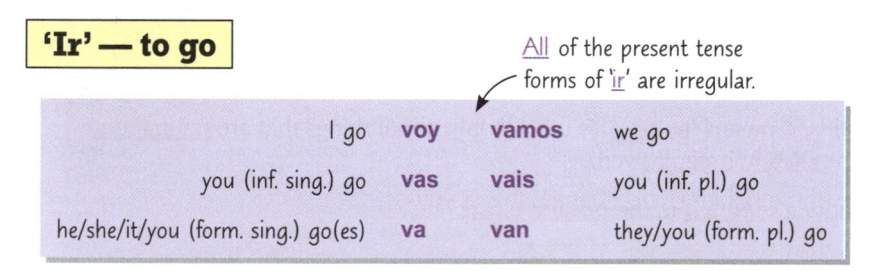

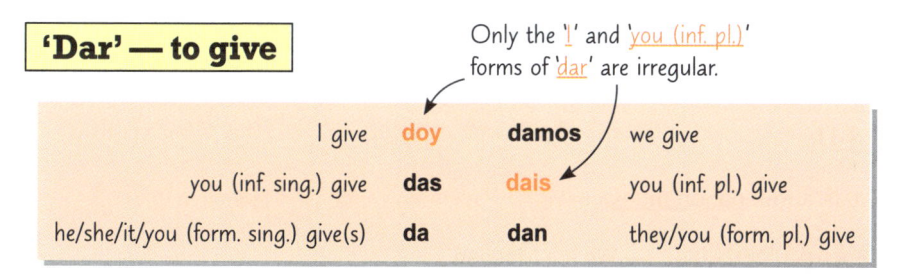

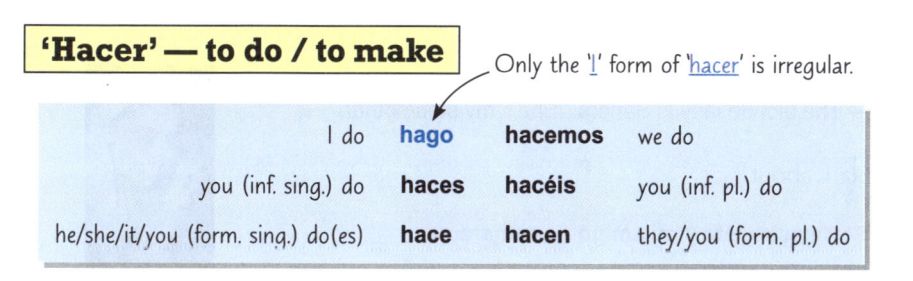

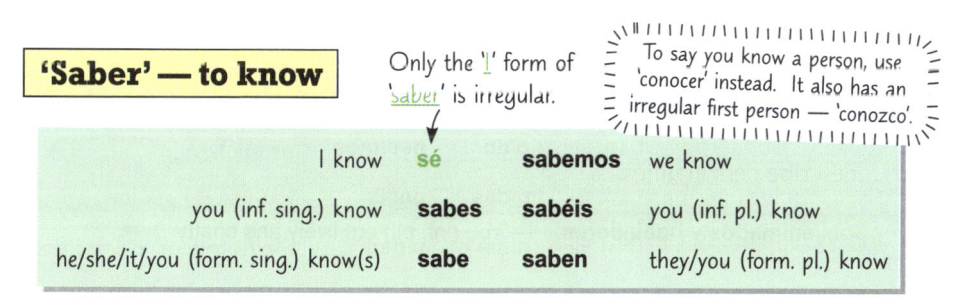

'Ir' — to go

All of the present tense forms of 'ir' are irregular.

I go	**voy**	**vamos**	we go
you (inf. sing.) go	**vas**	**vais**	you (inf. pl.) go
he/she/it/you (form. sing.) go(es)	**va**	**van**	they/you (form. pl.) go

'Dar' — to give

Only the 'I' and 'you (inf. pl.)' forms of 'dar' are irregular.

I give	**doy**	**damos**	we give
you (inf. sing.) give	**das**	**dais**	you (inf. pl.) give
he/she/it/you (form. sing.) give(s)	**da**	**dan**	they/you (form. pl.) give

'Hacer' — to do / to make

Only the 'I' form of 'hacer' is irregular.

I do	**hago**	**hacemos**	we do
you (inf. sing.) do	**haces**	**hacéis**	you (inf. pl.) do
he/she/it/you (form. sing.) do(es)	**hace**	**hacen**	they/you (form. pl.) do

'Saber' — to know

Only the 'I' form of 'saber' is irregular.

To say you know a person, use 'conocer' instead. It also has an irregular first person — 'conozco'.

I know	**sé**	**sabemos**	we know
you (inf. sing.) know	**sabes**	**sabéis**	you (inf. pl.) know
he/she/it/you (form. sing.) know(s)	**sabe**	**saben**	they/you (form. pl.) know

'Ser' and 'Estar'

In Spanish, there are two verbs for 'to be' — 'ser' and 'estar'. They're used in different situations, so it's important that you know which is which.

Use 'ser' for permanent things

The verb 'ser' means 'to be'. It's used to talk about things that are permanent. It is a completely irregular verb.

Here's how it's formed in the present tense:

I am	**soy**	**somos**	we are
you (inf. sing.) are	**eres**	**sois**	you (inf. pl.) are
he/she/it/you (form. sing.) is/are	**es**	**son**	they/you (form. pl.) are

It is used to...

1) ...talk about nationalities.

   Somos nigerianas. — We are Nigerian.

2) ...say someone's name or say who someone is in relation to you.

   La rubia es Sandra. Es mi madrastra.
   — The blonde lady is Sandra. She's my stepmother.

3) ...talk about jobs.

   Soy electricista y mi amigo es camarero.
   — I am an electrician and my friend is a waiter.

4) ...describe physical characteristics of a person or thing.

   Son de altura mediana. — They are of medium height.

It was a bit late for Elvira's friends to tell her it was permanent...

5) ...describe personalities.

   Sois animados y habladores. — You (inf. pl.) are lively and chatty.

Section 5 — Verbs

Use 'estar' for temporary things and locations

The verb 'estar' also means 'to be'. It's used to talk about things that are temporary or to say where things are. It is also a completely irregular verb.

Here's how it's formed in the present tense:

I am	estoy	estamos	we are
you (inf. sing.) are	estás	estáis	you (inf. pl.) are
he/she/it/you (form. sing.) is/are	está	están	they/you (form. pl.) are

It is used to...

1) ...talk about things that might change in the future.

   Estoy contenta. — I am happy. ← At the moment you are, but you might not be in the future.

2) ...talk about where someone or something is.

   Nisha está en Cuba. — Nisha is in Cuba.

   Los pantalones están en mi armario. — The trousers are in my wardrobe.

'Ser' and 'estar' with adjectives

There are some adjectives that change their meaning depending on whether they're used with 'ser' or 'estar'.

With 'estar'	Meaning	With 'ser'	Meaning
Estar bueno/a	to be attractive	Ser bueno/a	to be good
Estar abierto/a	to be open (e.g. a door)	Ser abierto/a	to be an open person
Estar vivo/a	to be alive	Ser vivo/a	to be lively
Estar cansado/a	to be tired	Ser cansado/a	to be tiresome
Estar nuevo/a	to look/feel new	Ser nuevo/a	to be (brand) new
Estar rico/a	to be tasty (food)	Ser rico/a	to be rich

Reflexive Verbs

Reflexive verbs are often used when talking about your daily routine.

Reflexive verbs — verbs you do to yourself

1) Sometimes you'll have to talk about things you do to yourself — like 'washing yourself' or 'getting yourself up' in the morning.

2) To do this, you need to use a reflexive verb.

3) Reflexive verbs in Spanish are those with 'se' at the end, e.g. lavarse (to have a wash) — 'se' means 'oneself' and changes to match the person doing the action.

Mateo was more than happy to re-flex for the crowd.

'Me', 'te', 'se' — reflexive pronouns

1) Reflexive verbs usually follow a straightforward pattern.

2) You conjugate the verb as normal, then add a reflexive pronoun in front of it.

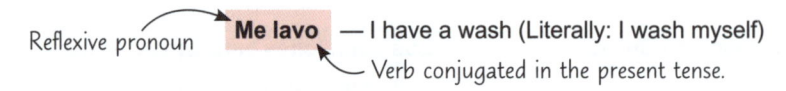

Reflexive pronoun → **Me lavo** — I have a wash (Literally: I wash myself)
↳ Verb conjugated in the present tense.

3) So, to use a reflexive verb in Spanish, you'll need to know the reflexive pronouns:

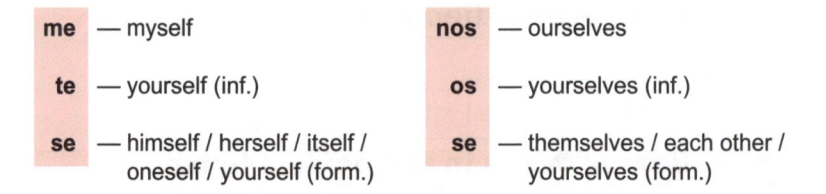

me	— myself	**nos**	— ourselves
te	— yourself (inf.)	**os**	— yourselves (inf.)
se	— himself / herself / itself / oneself / yourself (form.)	**se**	— themselves / each other / yourselves (form.)

'Me lavo' — I have a wash

Here's an example of a reflexive verb in action:

I have a wash	**me** lavo	**nos** lavamos	we have a wash
you (inf. sing.) have a wash	**te** lavas	**os** laváis	you (inf. pl.) have a wash
he/she/it has a wash / you (form. sing.) have a wash	**se** lava	**se** lavan	they/you (form. pl.) have a wash

Section 5 — Verbs

Learn these reflexive verbs

There are lots of reflexive verbs, but here are the ones you really should know:

English verb	Spanish verb	Example
to go to bed	acostarse	¿A qué hora te acuestas? (What time do you go to bed?)
to get up	levantarse	Ella se levanta temprano. (She gets up early.)
to feel	sentirse	¿Cómo te sientes? (How do you feel?)
to be called	llamarse	Me llamo Clarice. (I'm called Clarice.)
to wake up	despertarse	Se despiertan a las siete. (They wake up at 7 o'clock.)
to leave	irse	Se van en dos horas. (They are leaving in two hours.)
to get dressed	vestirse	Nos vestimos rápidamente. (We get dressed quickly.)
to put on	ponerse	Me pongo el uniforme escolar. (I put on my school uniform.)

Cuidado: 'Acostarse', 'sentirse', 'despertarse' and 'vestirse' are all radical-changing verbs (see p.44). 'Ponerse' is irregular in the first person 'I' form.

Putting reflexive verbs in the perfect tense

1) When you want to use reflexive verbs in the perfect tense (see p.56) to talk about things that have happened in the past, the structure is the same.

2) Put the reflexive pronoun (e.g. 'me', 'te', 'se') in front of the verb as usual:

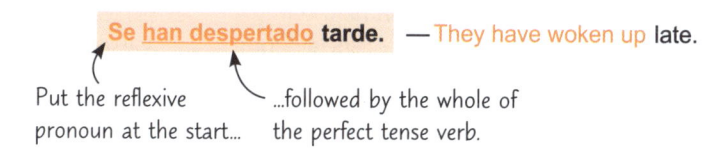

Se han despertado tarde. — They have woken up late.

Put the reflexive pronoun at the start... ...followed by the whole of the perfect tense verb.

Section 5 — Verbs

Preterite vs. Imperfect

The preterite tense and the imperfect tense are two ways of talking about the past — it's important to know which one to use.

The preterite tense is used to...

1) ...talk about a single completed action in the past.

   Empezaste tu empleo el miércoles. — **You started** your job on Wednesday.

2) ...talk about events that happened during a set period of time.

   El año pasado, fui a Cádiz. — Last year, I went to Cádiz.

3) ...interrupt a description of an action taking place in the imperfect tense.

   Comía un bocadillo cuando me caí. — I was eating a sandwich when I fell over.

The imperfect tense is used to...

1) ...talk about what you used to do repeatedly in the past.

   Viajaba mucho con mi empleo. — I used to travel a lot with my job.

2) ...describe something, like the weather, in the past.

   Era un día despejado y hacía sol. — It was a clear day and it was sunny.

3) ...talk about what was taking place when something else happened. You use the imperfect tense to describe the background situation.

   Leía mi libro cuando sonó el teléfono.
   — I was reading my book when the phone rang.

4) ...say how long something had been happening. For this, you also need 'desde hacía' (see p.55) which is the imperfect form of 'desde hace'.

   You only need to be able to recognise 'desde hacía' — you don't need to be able to use it.

   Vivía allí desde hacía tres años cuando me fui.
   — I had been living there for three years when I left.

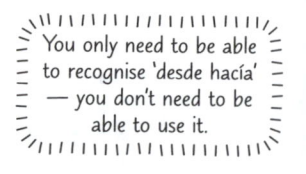

Section 5 — Verbs

Preterite Tense — Regular Verbs

Without further ado, here's how to form the preterite tense of regular verbs...

'-ar' verb endings

To form the preterite tense of regular '-ar' verbs, find the stem of the verb (see p.42) and add these endings:

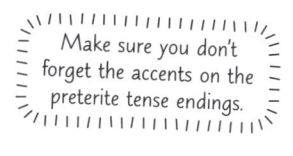

Make sure you don't forget the accents on the preterite tense endings.

I	-é	-amos	we
you (informal singular)	-aste	-asteis	you (informal plural)
he/she/it/you (formal singular)	-ó	-aron	they/you (formal plural)

La clase empezó a las nueve. — The class started at 9 o'clock.

El jueves, jugaron al baloncesto. — On Thursday, they played basketball.

But first, they had to learn how to dribble.

¿Aprovechaste del día? — Did you make the most of the day?

'-er' and '-ir' verb endings

The preterite tense of regular '-er' and '-ir' verbs is formed by adding these endings to the stem of the verb (see p.42):

I	-í	-imos	we
you (informal singular)	-iste	-isteis	you (informal plural)
he/she/it/you (formal singular)	-ió	-ieron	they/you (formal plural)

Corrieron a la escuela. — They ran to school.

Comimos la tarta de cumpleaños. — We ate the birthday cake.

Ayer, escribí una carta a mi tía. — Yesterday, I wrote a letter to my aunt.

Preterite Tense — Irregular Verbs

There are lots of irregular verbs in the preterite tense and they change in lots of different ways — make sure you learn them carefully.

'Ser' — to be

I was	fui	fuimos	we were
you (inf. sing.) were	fuiste	fuisteis	you (inf. pl.) were
he/she/it/you (form. sing.) was/were	fue	fueron	they/you (form. pl.) were

'Ir' — to go

In the preterite tense, the verbs 'ser' and 'ir' are the same.

I went	fui	fuimos	we went
you (inf. sing.) went	fuiste	fuisteis	you (inf. pl.) went
he/she/it/you (form. sing.) went	fue	fueron	they/you (form. pl.) went

'Estar' — to be

I was	estuve	estuvimos	we were
you (inf. sing.) were	estuviste	estuvisteis	you (inf. pl.) were
he/she/it/you (form. sing.) was/were	estuvo	estuvieron	they/you (form. pl.) were

'Hacer' — to do / to make

I did/made	hice	hicimos	we did/made
you (inf. sing.) did/made	hiciste	hicisteis	you (inf. pl.) did/made
he/she/it/you (form. sing.) did/made	hizo	hicieron	they/you (form. pl.) did/made

Section 5 — Verbs

Verbs ending in '-car' and '-zar'

To keep the correct pronunciation in the preterite tense, verbs ending in '-car' and '-zar' change their spelling in the first person ('I') form. For example:

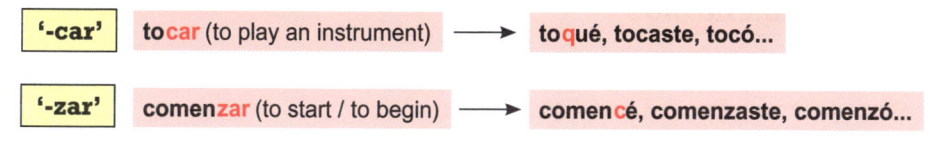

| '-car' | tocar (to play an instrument) | → | toqué, tocaste, tocó... |

| '-zar' | comenzar (to start / to begin) | → | comencé, comenzaste, comenzó... |

Verbs can change their stems in the preterite

1) Some verbs change their stem in the preterite tense and lose the accents in the 'I' and 'he/she/it/you (form. sing.)' forms.

2) There are lots of verbs that act like this, but here are some useful ones:

Verb	Stem	Example
dar (to give)	di-	Juan me dio un anillo. (Juan gave me a ring.)
decir (to say)	dij-	¿Dijiste algo? (Did you say something?)
poder (to be able to)	pud-	Pude volver. (I was able to go back.)
poner (to put)	pus-	Lo puse en la mesa. (I put it on the table.)
querer (to want)	quis-	Mila quiso gritar. (Mila wanted to scream.)
tener (to have)	tuv-	Tuvimos suerte. (We were lucky.)
traer (to bring)	traj-	Trajo la cuenta. (He / She brought the bill.)
venir (to come)	vin-	Vinieron a clase. (They came to class.)

3) Verbs derived from these irregular verbs follow the same patterns:

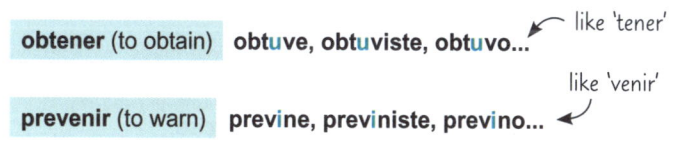

obtener (to obtain)   obtuve, obtuviste, obtuvo...   ← like 'tener'

prevenir (to warn)   previne, previniste, previno...   ← like 'venir'

Imperfect Tense

The imperfect tense helps you talk about what you 'were doing', what 'was happening' and what you 'used to do'. (See p.50 for more on the imperfect).

'-ar' verb endings

To form the imperfect tense of regular '-ar' verbs, find the stem of the verb (see p.42) and add these endings: — Don't forget this accent.

	I	we	
I	-aba	-ábamos	we
you (informal singular)	-abas	-abais	you (informal plural)
he/she/it/you (formal singular)	-aba	-aban	they/you (formal plural)

Gastábamos demasiado dinero.
— We were spending too much money.

Cuidaba de él.
— I was looking after him.

'-er' and '-ir' verb endings

The endings for '-er' and '-ir' verbs all have accents.

Add these endings to the stem of the verb (p.42) to form the imperfect tense of regular '-er' and '-ir' verbs:

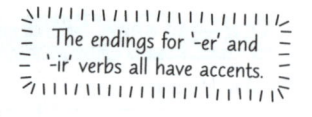

	I		we
I	-ía	-íamos	we
you (informal singular)	-ías	-íais	you (informal plural)
he/she/it/you (formal singular)	-ía	-ían	they/you (formal plural)

Comían mucha comida basura.
— They were eating lots of junk food.

Dante escribía libros.
— Dante was writing books.

Use 'solía' to say what you 'used to do'

You can also say what you used to do using the imperfect tense of the verb 'soler' and the infinitive.

Solía hacer mucho ejercicio. — I used to do a lot of exercise.

Solíamos ir al parque cada sábado. — We used to go to the park every Saturday.

'Ser', 'ir' and 'ver' are irregular

'Ser' — to be

I was	era	éramos	we were
you (inf. sing.) were	eras	erais	you (inf. pl.) were
he/she/it/you (form. sing.) was/were	era	eran	they/you (form. pl.) were

'Ir' — to go

I went	iba	íbamos	we went
you (inf. sing.) went	ibas	ibais	you (inf. pl.) went
he/she/it/you (form. sing.) went	iba	iban	they/you (form. pl.) went

'Ver' — to see

The stem of the verb 'ver' changes to 've-' in the imperfect tense, but it still takes the regular '-er' verb endings:

ver (to see) ⟶ **veía, veías, veía, veíamos, veíais, veían**

'Había' means 'there was' or 'there were'

1) In the present tense, 'hay' means 'there is' or 'there are'.
2) The imperfect form of 'hay' is 'había', which means 'there was' or 'there were'.
3) 'Había' stays the same, whether the noun is singular or plural.

Use 'desde hacía' to talk about how long

Use 'desde hacía' to talk about how long something had been happening for when something else happened.

Jugaba desde hacía media hora cuando me hice daño.
— I had been playing for half an hour when I injured myself.

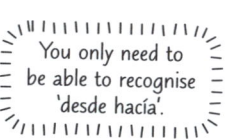

You only need to be able to recognise 'desde hacía'.

Section 5 — Verbs

Perfect Tense

Use the perfect tense to say what you 'have done'

1) The perfect tense lets you talk about things that you 'have done' in the past.

2) To form the perfect tense in English, you use the correct form of 'have' to match the subject, along with the past participle (see p.57):

I have skated.
'I' form of 'have' — past participle of 'to skate'

3) In the perfect tense, past participles don't change to agree in number or in gender with the person doing the action.

I have painted my nails perfectly.

'He hecho' — 'I have done'

1) The perfect tense in Spanish is made up of the correct form of the present tense of the verb 'haber' and the past participle (see p.57):

present tense of 'haber' + **past participle**

2) This is the present tense of 'haber':

I have...	**he**	**hemos**	we have...
you (inf. sing.) have...	**has**	**habéis**	you (inf. pl.) have...
he/she/it/you (form. sing.) have...	**ha**	**han**	they/you (form. pl.) have...

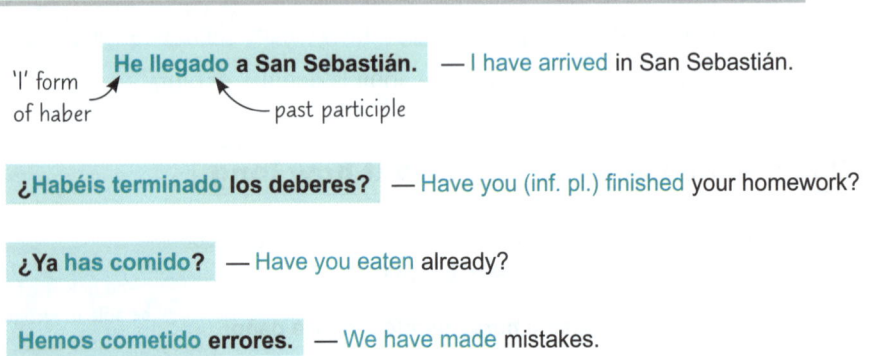

He llegado a San Sebastián. — I have arrived in San Sebastián.
'I' form of haber ↗ ↘ past participle

¿Habéis terminado los deberes? — Have you (inf. pl.) finished your homework?

¿Ya has comido? — Have you eaten already?

Hemos cometido errores. — We have made mistakes.

Section 5 — Verbs

Past Participles

Most past participles are regular

1) You need the past participle to form the perfect tense (see p.56) and pluperfect tense (see p.58) in Spanish.

2) To form the past participle of:

'-ar' verbs:
> REMOVE '-AR' + ADD '-ADO'
> e.g. **cancelar** (to cancel) — **cancelado** (cancelled)

'-er' and '-ir' verbs:
> REMOVE '-ER' OR '-IR' + ADD '-IDO'
> e.g. **querer** (to want) — **querido** (wanted)
> **decidir** (to decide) — **decidido** (decided)

EXCEPTIONS

Not all verbs follow these rules though. There are some irregular past participles that you also need to know:

Verb	Past participle
abrir (to open)	abierto (opened)
cubrir (to cover)	cubierto (covered)
decir (to say)	dicho (said)
escribir (to write)	escrito (written)
hacer (to do / to make)	hecho (done / made)
leer (to read)	leído (read)
poner (to put)	puesto (put)
romper (to break)	roto (broken)
ver (to see)	visto (seen)
volver (to return)	vuelto (returned)

Section 5 — Verbs

Pluperfect Tense

Use the pluperfect tense to say what you 'had done'

1) The pluperfect tense is similar to the perfect tense (see p.56).
2) While the perfect tense is for things that you have done, the pluperfect tense is for things that you had done.

> The waiter cleared our plates when I had finished eating.
> past tense of 'I have'   past participle of 'to finish'

'Había hecho' — 'I had done'

1) The pluperfect tense in Spanish is formed in the same way as the perfect tense, but it uses the imperfect tense of 'haber':

imperfect tense of 'haber' + past participle

2) Here is the imperfect tense of 'haber':

I had...	había	habíamos	we had...
you (inf. sing.) had...	habías	habíais	you (inf. pl.) had...
he/she/it/you (form. sing.) had...	había	habían	they/you (form. pl.) had...

Había llamado a mi madre. — I had called my mother.

Habíamos vuelto a casa. — We had returned home.

Ya habías salido cuando llegaron. — You had already left when they arrived.

Reshmi no había lavado los platos.
— Reshmi hadn't washed the dishes.

Nunca habían visto a Rafael.
— They had never seen Rafael.

With negative sentences, the negative word goes before 'haber' and the past participle.

Section 5 — Verbs

Immediate Future Tense

The immediate future tense is for talking about what you're going to do.

'I am going to...'

1) To talk about future actions, you need to use the future tense.
2) In Spanish, there are two future tenses that you need to know — the immediate future and the proper future (see p.60).
3) The immediate future can be used to talk about something that's about to happen, as well as something you intend to do in the future. It usually refers to what you're going to do:

I am going to go for a run.

We are going to learn Korean.

"I said I was going to go — I didn't say when."

'Ir a' plus the infinitive

To form the immediate future in Spanish, take the present tense form of the verb 'ir' (to go), then add 'a' and a verb in the infinitive (see p.41).

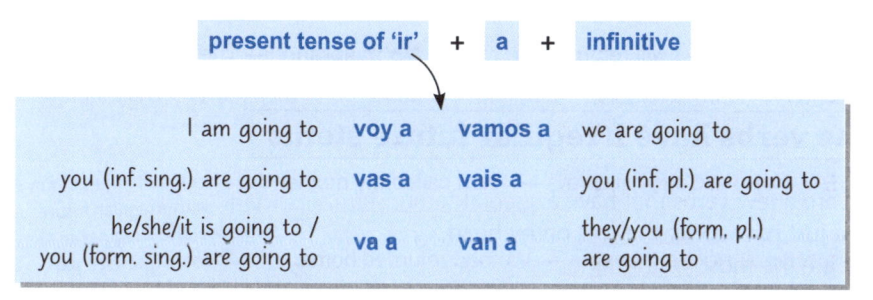

present tense of 'ir' + a + infinitive

I am going to	voy a	vamos a	we are going to
you (inf. sing.) are going to	vas a	vais a	you (inf. pl.) are going to
he/she/it is going to / you (form. sing.) are going to	va a	van a	they/you (form. pl.) are going to

Vamos a salir a las ocho. — We are going to leave at 8 o'clock.

Van a casarse en Lisboa. — They are going to get married in Lisbon.

¿Quién va a reservar la mesa? — Who is going to book the table?

Mañana, voy a almorzar fuera. — Tomorrow, I am going to have lunch outside.

Section 5 — Verbs

Proper Future Tense

The proper future tense is slightly different to the immediate future tense — it is used to say what will happen:

He will apologise for his mistake.

If we don't leave soon, we will be late.

Add the future tense endings to the infinitive

To form the proper future tense of regular verbs, add the future endings to the infinitive. These endings are the same for all verbs.

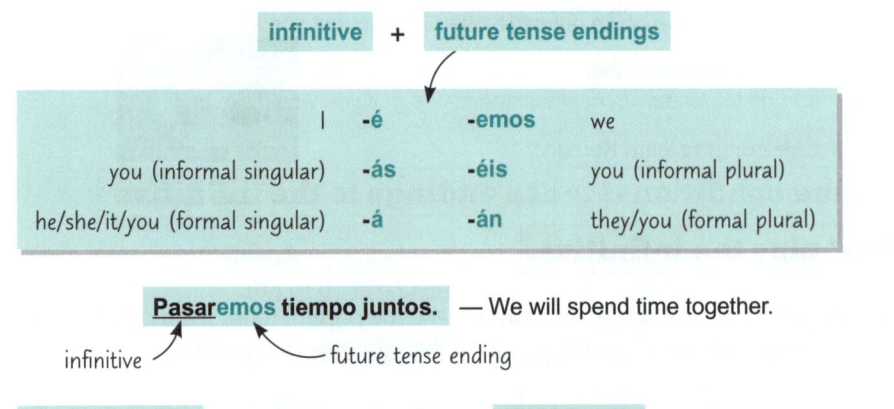

infinitive + future tense endings

I	-é	-emos	we
you (informal singular)	-ás	-éis	you (informal plural)
he/she/it/you (formal singular)	-á	-án	they/you (formal plural)

Pasaremos tiempo juntos. — We will spend time together.

infinitive ↗ ↖ future tense ending

Volveré a casa. — I will return home.

No bailarán. — They will not dance.

Some verbs have irregular future stems

There are a few verbs that have a special future stem, so you just have to learn them off by heart. These are the most important ones:

Verbs with irregular future stems are also irregular in the conditional tense (see p.61).

Infinitive	Future stem	Infinitive	Future stem
decir (to say)	dir-	**querer** (to want)	querr-
haber (to have...)	habr-	**saber** (to know)	sabr-
hacer (to do / to make)	har-	**venir** (to come)	vendr-
tener (to have)	tendr-	**poder** (to be able to)	podr-
poner (to put)	pondr-	**salir** (to go out)	saldr-

Section 5 — Verbs

Conditional Tense

If you want to talk about something in the future that might or might not happen, you use the conditional tense.

'Would', 'could', 'should'

The conditional tense in English usually involves the words 'would', 'could' or 'should' — these words show that the outcome is dependent on something else.

I **would** eat curry every day... (e.g. but I'm too busy to make it.)

She **should** take the rubbish out more often... (e.g. but she's too lazy.)

We **could** go to Venezuela next summer... (e.g. if you would like to.)

Add the conditional tense endings to the infinitive

To form the conditional tense, add the endings below to the infinitive. For irregular verbs, add the ending to the irregular stem (p.60).

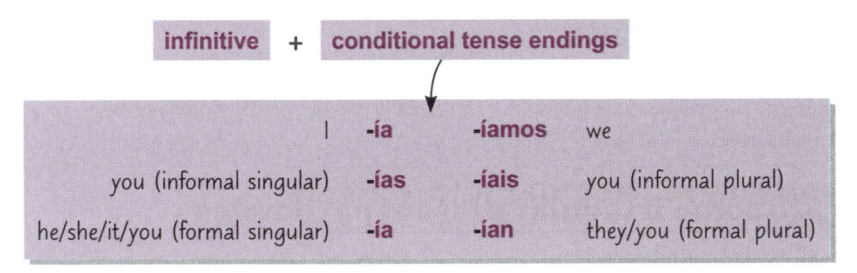

infinitive + conditional tense endings

I	-ía	-íamos	we	
you (informal singular)	-ías	-íais	you (informal plural)	
he/she/it/you (formal singular)	-ía	-ían	they/you (formal plural)	

Preferiríamos salir mañana. — We would prefer to go out tomorrow.

¿**Podrías** ayudarme? — Could you help me?

The conditional form of 'querer' ('querría') is often replaced by the imperfect subjunctive form ('quisiera') — see p.71.

Deberían llegar pronto. — They should arrive soon.

!Cuidado The conditional tense endings are the same as the imperfect tense endings for '-er' and '-ir' verbs. They are added to the infinitive, not the stem, so be careful not to get them mixed up.

Verbs with '-ing'

Verbs with '-ing' are used in the continuous tenses

1) <u>Usually</u>, when you translate phrases such as '<u>I am living</u>' or '<u>I was living</u>', you'd use the <u>normal tenses</u> — 'I am living' would be '<u>vivo</u>' (present tense) and 'I was living' would be '<u>vivía</u>' (imperfect tense).

2) However, if you want to <u>stress</u> that something <u>is happening right now</u> or was happening <u>at a specific moment</u> in the <u>past</u>, you need to use the <u>continuous tenses</u>.

3) These tenses talk about <u>ongoing actions</u> and are made up of the verb '<u>estar</u>' and the <u>present participle</u>.

The present participle is the '-ing' part

The present participle is also called the 'gerund'.

To form the <u>present participle</u> of the verb, find its <u>stem</u> (<u>p.42</u>) and add the correct <u>ending</u>:

For '-<u>ar</u>' verbs, add '-<u>ando</u>'.

e.g. hablar (to speak) → hablando
cantar (to sing) → cantando

For '-<u>er</u>' and '-<u>ir</u>' verbs, add '-<u>iendo</u>'.

e.g. beber (to drink) → bebiendo
salir (to go out) → saliendo

There are some irregular present participles

There are a few <u>irregulars</u> that you <u>need to know</u>, so make sure you're comfortable with them:

Infinitive	Present participle	Infinitive	Present participle
caer (to fall)	cayendo	servir (to serve)	sirviendo
leer (to read)	leyendo	pedir (to ask for)	pidiendo
oír (to hear)	oyendo	morir (to die)	muriendo
construir (to build)	construyendo	decir (to say)	diciendo
ir (to go)	yendo	dormir (to sleep)	durmiendo

Section 5 — Verbs

The present continuous is for what is happening now

1) To form the present continuous, take the present tense of 'estar' and the present participle.

2) Present participles don't change to agree with the subject.

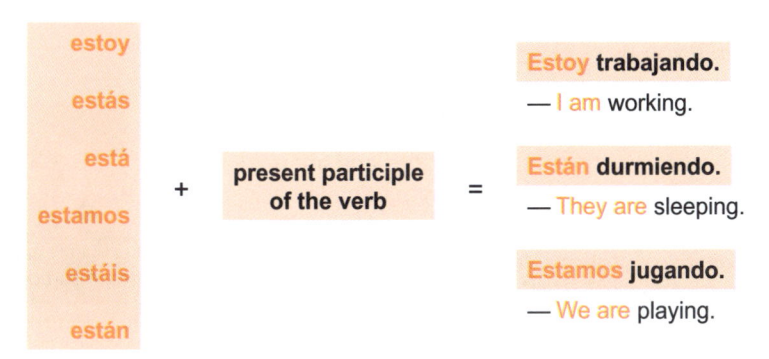

estoy		Estoy trabajando.
estás		— I am working.
está	+ present participle of the verb =	Están durmiendo.
estamos		— They are sleeping.
estáis		Estamos jugando.
están		— We are playing.

The imperfect continuous is for what was happening

1) The imperfect continuous is formed in the same way as the present continuous, but 'estar' has to be in the imperfect tense.

I was	estaba	estábamos	we were
you (inf. sing.) were	estabas	estabais	you (inf. pl.) were
he/she/it/you (form. sing.) was/were	estaba	estaban	they/you (form. pl.) were

Estabas leyendo una revista. — You were reading a magazine.

2) The imperfect continuous is particularly useful when you want to say what you were doing when something else happened.

Estaba levantando la mano cuando contestó María.
— I was putting my hand up when María answered.

3) The use of continuous tenses is more common in English than in Spanish — if in doubt, use the present or imperfect tense instead.

Section 5 — Verbs

Negatives

There are lots of different ways to express negatives in Spanish — you need to be able to understand them all, and it looks great if you can use them too.

'No' means 'no' and 'not'

1) To make a sentence negative in Spanish, you have to put 'no' in front of the verb and any object pronouns in the sentence.

   No es hombre de negocios. — He is not a businessman.

   No lo tengo. — I don't have it.

2) To ask negative questions, 'no' follows the same rule — it goes before the verb and any object pronouns.

   ¿No te vas a ir? — Aren't you going to go?

   Alvaro couldn't believe they'd seen through his disguise.

3) To answer questions in Spanish, you might need to say 'no' twice:

   No, no conozco a Marisol. — No, I don't know Marisol.

'No' is the most common negative word

1) As well as in questions, you can also use '¿no?' after a statement — it invites the person you are addressing to respond to the statement with a yes or no answer.

   Te gustan los calamares, ¿no? — You like squid, don't you?

2) Negative constructions work the same in all the different tenses.

   No hicieron los deberes. — They didn't do the homework.

   No perderé el tren. — I won't miss the train.

   Cuando hablamos con Paquita, no sabía las buenas noticias.
   — When we spoke to Paquita, she didn't know the good news.

Section 5 — Verbs

There are lots more useful negatives

1) There are lots of negative constructions — helpfully, most start with 'no'.
2) To say things like 'nobody' and 'nothing', you use different negative words with 'no'. 'No' stays in front of the verb, and the other negative word goes after.
3) 'Nunca' is a bit different — it can also go on its own at the start of a sentence.

English negative	Spanish negative	Example
no longer (not any more)	ya no	Ya no como carne. (I no longer eat meat. / I don't eat meat any more.)
nobody (not anybody)	no ... nadie	No conozco a nadie. (I know nobody. / I don't know anybody.)
never (not ever)	no ... nunca / jamás nunca...	No volveré nunca / jamás. Nunca volveré. (I'll never go back. / I won't ever go back.)
nothing (not anything)	no ... nada	No comimos nada. (We ate nothing. / We didn't eat anything.)
neither ... nor	no ... ni ... ni	No fueron ni a Chile ni a Uruguay. (They went neither to Chile nor to Uruguay.)

When 'ni' is used more than once in a sentence, it goes before each full item, including any prepositions.

EXCEPTIONS

1) 'Ninguno/a' behaves slightly differently.
2) It is formed in the same way — it goes after the verb, which is preceded by 'no', but it has different uses.
3) It can be used as both a pronoun (to replace the noun) and an adjective (before the noun).
4) It agrees with the noun in the sentence and changes when it is used as a pronoun before a masculine noun:

'Ninguno/a' is almost always used in the singular form. You don't need to worry about the plural.

English negative	Spanish negative	Example
not a single... (none / not one)	no ... ningún/ninguna	No tengo ningún problema. (I don't have a single problem.)
not a single one (none / not one)	no ... ninguno/a	No han visto ninguna. (They haven't seen a single one.)

adjective → (first row)
pronoun → (second row)

Section 5 — Verbs

Passive

Sentences can be active or passive

1) In active sentences, the action is done to the object.

   'Akhil' is doing the action — he's the subject.

   Akhil stroked the toad.

   'The toad' is having the action done to it — it's the object.

2) In passive sentences, the action is done to the subject.

   'The toad' is the subject, even though the action is being done to it.

   The toad was stroked by Akhil.

3) You don't need to be able to use the passive in Spanish, but you do need to be able to recognise it.

Subject + 'ser' + past participle — Spanish passive

1) The passive in Spanish is made up of a person or a thing (the subject), plus 'ser' (to be), plus the past participle (see p.57):

   PASSIVE = SUBJECT + SER + PAST PARTICIPLE

2) The past participle must agree with the subject having the action done to it:

   past participle

   Las verduras son lavadas. — The vegetables are washed.

   Third person plural form of 'ser'

   'Las verduras' is feminine so 'lavadas' agrees.

3) The 'ser' part can change tense:

   Las verduras fueron lavadas. — The vegetables were washed.

   Las verduras serán lavadas. — The vegetables will be washed.

Use 'por' to show who's doing the action

If you want to say who or what is doing the action, add it after 'por' (by).

La pelota fue tirada por Nancy. — The ball was thrown by Nancy.

Section 5 — Verbs

Impersonal Verbs

Impersonal verbs only work in the third person

1) Impersonal verbs refer to things generally, without a specific subject pronoun. They only work with the third person (it / they) forms of the verb.

2) Here's an example of an impersonal verb:

   Se puede alquilar un coche. — One can hire a car.

3) You can turn any Spanish verb into an impersonal verb (e.g. 'one does' rather than 'I do') by using 'se' and the 'it' or 'they' form of the verb.

   Ahora, se habla de la pobreza. — Nowadays, there is talk of poverty.

4) If there's a singular subject in the sentence, use the 'it' form of the verb, and use the 'they' form for plural subjects.

   La tienda se cierra desde la una a las dos. — The shop is closed from 1 until 2.

   Se construyen muchas casas aquí. — Lots of houses are built here.

Some important impersonal verbs

1) 'Hay que' is an impersonal way of saying 'one has to do something'.

   Hay que reciclar latas. — One has to recycle tins.

2) 'Parece que' means 'it seems that'.

   Parece que nadie sabe qué hacer. — It seems that nobody knows what to do.

3) Weather verbs are always impersonal.

   Nieva mucho en el norte. — It snows a lot in the north.

   Llueve desde ayer. — It's been raining since yesterday.

   You couldn't say 'I snow' or 'we rain', for example. They just don't make sense.

Section 5 — Verbs

Subjunctive

Some impersonal verbs (see p.67) and phrases in Spanish are followed by the subjunctive. You need to know when to use it and how to form it.

Use the present subjunctive...

1) ...to get someone else to do something:

   Quiero que pases la aspiradora. — I want you to do the vacuum cleaning.

2) ...to express a wish or desire:

   Esperamos que os gusten. — We hope that you (inf. pl.) like them.

3) ...after expressing an emotion or opinion:

   No creo que sea necesario. — I don't believe that it is necessary.

4) ...to say that something's unlikely to happen:

   Es poco probable que estén de acuerdo. — It's unlikely that they will agree.

5) ...when there's a requirement:

   Busco una casa que tenga jardín. — I'm looking for a house that has a garden.

6) ...after 'cuando' (when), 'antes de que' (before) and 'aunque' (even if) when talking about the future:

   Vamos a la playa aunque llueva. — We're going to the beach even if it rains.

7) ...after 'para que' (so that) to express purpose:

   Abre la puerta para que pueda entrar. — Open the door so that I can come in.

8) ...in negative opinions:

   No creo que ellas vengan a la fiesta. — I don't think they are coming to the party

Section 5 — Verbs

Forming the present subjunctive

1) The subjunctive is formed using the stem from the 'I' form of the present tense.
2) For '-ar' verbs, add the '-er' present tense endings. For '-er' and '-ir' verbs, add the '-ar' endings.

This Valentine's present from Ana was making Amy quite tense.

infinitive	hablar	comer	vivir
'yo' form	hablo	como	vivo
I	hable	coma	viva
you (inf. sing.)	hables	comas	vivas
he/she/it/you (form. sing.)	hable	coma	viva
we	hablemos	comamos	vivamos
you (inf. pl.)	habléis	comáis	viváis
they/you (form. pl.)	hablen	coman	vivan

Irregular verbs in the present subjunctive

Some verbs are irregular in the 'I' form in the present tense, so the subjunctive has to match this.

'Poder' — to be able to

'Poder' is a radical-changing verb, so its 'we' and 'you (inf. pl.)' forms have regular stems.

I can	pueda	podamos	we can
you (inf. sing.) can	puedas	podáis	you (inf. pl.) can
he/she/it/you (form. sing.) can	pueda	puedan	they/you (form. pl.) can

'Tener' — to have

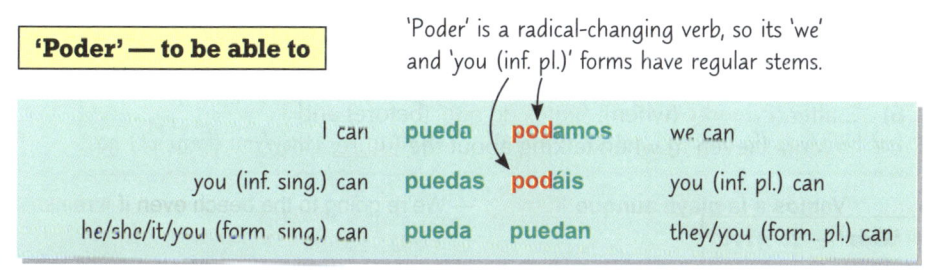

'Hacer' and 'venir' also follow this pattern.

I have	tenga	tengamos	we have
you (inf. sing.) have	tengas	tengáis	you (inf. pl.) have
he/she/it/you (form. sing.) has/have	tenga	tengan	they/you (form. pl.) have

Section 5 — Verbs

Subjunctive

Some verbs are completely irregular

The verbs 'ser', 'estar', 'ir', and 'dar' are completely irregular in the present subjunctive — you'll need to learn these off by heart.

'Ser' — to be

I am	**sea**	**seamos**	we are
you (inf. sing.) are	**seas**	**seáis**	you (inf. pl.) are
he/she/it/you (form. sing.) is/are	**sea**	**sean**	they/you (form. pl.) are

'Estar' — to be

I am	**esté**	**estemos**	we are
you (inf. sing.) are	**estés**	**estéis**	you (inf. pl.) are
he/she/it/you (form. sing.) is/are	**esté**	**estén**	they/you (form. pl.) are

'Ir' — to go

I go	**vaya**	**vayamos**	we go
you (inf. sing.) go	**vayas**	**vayáis**	you (inf. pl.) go
he/she/it/you (form. sing.) go(es)	**vaya**	**vayan**	they/you (form. pl.) go

'Dar' — to give

I give	**dé**	**demos**	we give
you (inf. sing.) give	**des**	**deis**	you (inf. pl.) give
he/she/it/you (form. sing.) give(s)	**dé**	**den**	they/you (form. pl.) give

Section 5 — Verbs

Imperfect Subjunctive

Hold onto your hats, there's also an imperfect subjunctive in Spanish...

Forming the imperfect subjunctive

1) You don't need to be able to use the imperfect subjunctive (apart from 'quisiera' below), but you do need to be able to recognise it.

2) The imperfect subjunctive uses the same stem as the present subjunctive but has different endings:

	hablar	comer	vivir
I	hablara	comiera	viviera
you (inf. sing.)	hablaras	comieras	vivieras
he/she/it/you (form. sing.)	hablara	comiera	viviera
we	habláramos	comiéramos	viviéramos
you (inf. pl.)	hablarais	comierais	vivierais
they/you (form. pl.)	hablaran	comieran	vivieran

Era vital que llegáramos a tiempo. — It was vital that we arrived on time.

Deseaban que fuera a la universidad. — They wanted me to go to university.

3) It's used in the same situations as the present subjunctive (see p.68), but it refers to things that have happened in the past.

'Quisiera...' — 'I would like...'

1) 'Quisiera' (I would like) is a common example of the imperfect subjunctive — you need to be able to recognise and use it.

2) It's often used instead of the conditional form of 'querer' ('querría') to say what you would like.

Quisiera dos kilos de patatas. — I would like two kilos of potatoes.

3) You might also see the imperfect subjunctive form of 'haber' ('hubiera') used instead of its conditional form 'habría'.

Lo hubiera comprado. — I would have bought it.

Section 5 — Verbs

Imperative

The imperative is for orders and requests

1) Sometimes you need to be able to give an order or make a request:

   Go away!   Please put your litter in the bin.   Help me!

2) This is called the imperative.
3) In Spanish, there are informal and formal forms of the imperative.

Informal commands

1) To form a singular informal command, take the '-s' off the 'tú' form of the present tense verb.

   hablas (you talk) → ¡Habla! (Talk!)

2) There are some common irregular imperatives:

Infinitive	Command (inf. sing.)
decir (to say)	¡Di! (Say!)
hacer (to do / to make)	¡Haz! (Do! / Make!)
ir (to go)	¡Ve! (Go!)
poner (to put)	¡Pon! (Put!)
salir (to go out)	¡Sal! (Go out!)
ser (to be)	¡Sé! (Be!)
tener (to have)	¡Ten! (Have!)
venir (to come)	¡Ven! (Come!)

Geoffrey had an informal approach to his boss's orders.

3) To tell two or more people what to do in an informal way, change the final '-r' of the infinitive to a '-d'.

   ¡Mirad! — Look!   ¡Escribid! — Write!   ¡Corred! — Run!

4) With positive commands, pronouns (e.g. me, them, it) are placed at the end of the word and you need to add an accent to show where the stress is.

   ¡Tráelo! — Bring it!   ¡Escúchame! — Listen to me!

Section 5 — Verbs

Formal commands

1) To politely tell someone what to do, use the formal 'you' singular form of the present subjunctive.

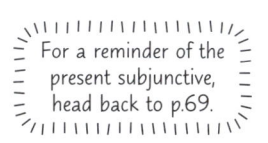

   ¡Cocine! — Cook!   ¡Lea! — Read!

   For a reminder of the present subjunctive, head back to p.69.

2) As always, there are some irregular forms that you'll need to learn:

Infinitive	Present subjunctive
dar (to give)	¡Dé! (Give!)
haber (to have...)	¡Haya! (Have!)
ir (to go)	¡Vaya! (Go!)
saber (to know)	¡Sepa! (Know!)
ser (to be)	¡Sea! (Be!)

3) When politely telling more than one person what to do, use the formal 'you' plural of the present subjunctive.

   ¡Sigan! — Follow!   ¡Salgan! — Go out!

   Cojan la segunda calle a la izquierda. — Take the second street on the left.

Making commands negative

1) To tell someone not to do something, always use the subjunctive.

   ¡No hables! — Don't speak!   ¡No comas! — Don't eat!

2) Watch out — any pronouns have to go before the verb.

   ¡Piérdelo! — Lose it!   ⟶   ¡No lo pierdas! — Don't lose it!

   ¡Evítale! — Avoid him!   ⟶   ¡No le evites! — Don't avoid him!

Asking Questions

Knowing how to ask questions is really useful if you want to ace your speaking test.

Raising your intonation can form a question

1) The simplest way to form a question in Spanish is by adding an upside down question mark at the beginning of a statement and a normal one at the end.

2) If you're speaking, raise the intonation in your voice at the end of the sentence.

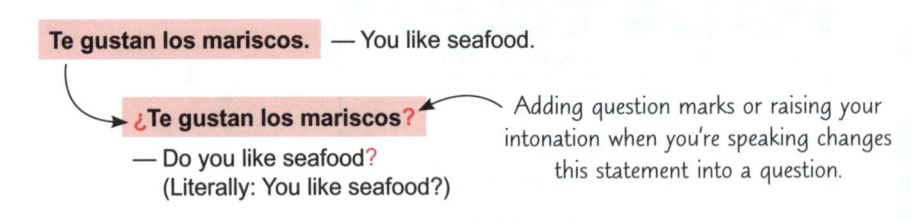

Te gustan los mariscos. — You like seafood.

¿Te gustan los mariscos?
— Do you like seafood?
(Literally: You like seafood?)

Adding question marks or raising your intonation when you're speaking changes this statement into a question.

Use these question words to form questions

1) You can also use question words like '¿Cuándo...' (When...), '¿Quién...' (Who...) and '¿Dónde...' (Where...) to ask questions, just like in English.

¿Cuándo quieres partir? — When do you want to leave?

¿Quién rompió los platos? — Who broke the plates?

¿Dónde están las llaves? — Where are the keys?

"You'll never find us! MWA HA HA HA!"

2) Other question words include '¿Por qué...' (Why...), '¿Qué...' (What...) and '¿Cómo...' (How...).

¿Por qué no viniste con nosotros? — Why didn't you come with us?

¿Qué haces los fines de semana? — What do you do at the weekends?

¿Cómo sabes lo que ocurrió? — How do you know what happened?

Section 5 — Verbs

Section 6 — Other Useful Stuff

Numbers

They might seem basic, but numbers are important.

Uno, dos, tres — one, two, three

1) You probably know the Spanish numbers by now, but here's a quick reminder:

'Uno' changes to 'un' before masculine nouns, e.g. 'un zapato' (a shoe) and 'una' before feminine nouns, e.g. 'una calabaza' (a pumpkin).

1	uno				
2	dos	11	once		
3	tres	12	doce	20	veinte
4	cuatro	13	trece	30	treinta
5	cinco	14	catorce	40	cuarenta
6	seis	15	quince	50	cincuenta
7	siete	16	dieciséis	60	sesenta
8	ocho	17	diecisiete	70	setenta
9	nueve	18	dieciocho	80	ochenta
10	diez	19	diecinueve	90	noventa

100	cien(to)
1000	mil
1,000,000	un millón

'Cien' becomes 'ciento' when used in front of another number (except 'mil').

2) All twenty-something numbers are rolled into one:

| 21 | veintiuno | 22 | veintidós | 23 | veintitrés |

When 21 comes before a masculine noun, it gains an accent, e.g. 'veintiún petroleros'.

3) After 30, numbers are joined by 'y' (and), but written separately:

| 31 | treinta y uno | 47 | cuarenta y siete | 59 | cincuenta y nueve |

First, second, third — ordinal numbers

1) Ordinal numbers are numbers like 'first', 'second' and 'third'.
2) These words always end in '-o' for masculine things and '-a' for feminine things.

| 1st | primero/a | 3rd | tercero/a | 5th | quinto/a | 7th | séptimo/a | 9th | noveno/a |
| 2nd | segundo/a | 4th | cuarto/a | 6th | sexto/a | 8th | octavo/a | 10th | décimo/a |

3) 'Primero' and 'tercero' drop the final '-o' in front of masculine singular words:

| el primer día | — the first day | el tercer hombre | — the third man |

Dates, Days and Time

'La fecha' — the date

1) In Spanish, months are masculine and shouldn't have capital letters.

enero	— January	**mayo**	— May	**septiembre**	— September
febrero	— February	**junio**	— June	**octubre**	— October
marzo	— March	**julio**	— July	**noviembre**	— November
abril	— April	**agosto**	— August	**diciembre**	— December

2) To say 'the first' of a month in Spanish you can say 'el primero de'. For all the other dates, you have to say 'the two of' and 'the sixteen of'.

Es el primero de junio.
— It's the first of June.

Es el veintiocho de septiembre.
— It's the twenty-eighth of September.

'Los días de la semana' — the days of the week

The days of the week are also masculine in Spanish and are written in lower case.

lunes	Monday	**jueves**	Thursday	**sábado**	Saturday
martes	Tuesday	**viernes**	Friday	**domingo**	Sunday
miércoles	Wednesday				

'¿Qué hora es?' — What time is it?

1) To say 'at X o'clock', you need 'a':

'La' changes to 'las' for anything other than 'one o'clock'.

a la una — at one o'clock   **a las cinco** — at five o'clock

2) To say 'it's X o'clock', use 'es' for one o'clock and 'son' for every other hour:

Es la una. — It's one o'clock.   **Son las cinco.** — It's five o'clock.

3) To say something is 'past' the hour, use 'y' and for 'to' the hour, use 'menos'. A 'quarter' of an hour is 'cuarto' and 'half' an hour is 'media':

Es la una y diez.
— It's ten past one.

Son las tres menos cuarto.
— It's quarter to three.

Section 6 — Other Useful Stuff

Conjunctions

Conjunctions help you make longer and more complicated sentences.

Conjunctions are joining words

1) Conjunctions join clauses together to make longer sentences.
2) They usually go in between the two clauses.

> Iñigo likes crime dramas, **but** he hates soap operas.
> ⎣first clause   conjunction   second clause⎦

'Y' — and

1) '<u>Y</u>' means '<u>and</u>' — you use it just like you would in English.

> **Estudio alemán.** AND **Estudio arte.**
> — I study German.   — I study art.
>   conjunction
>   'and'
> **Estudio alemán y arte.**
> — I study German and art.

2) '<u>Y</u>' changes to '<u>e</u>' before a word starting with '<u>i</u>' or '<u>hi</u>'.

> **Compré unos huevos, e hice un pastel.**
> — I bought some eggs, and I made a cake.

"Is this how it's supposed to look?"

'O' — or

1) '<u>O</u>' means '<u>or</u>'.

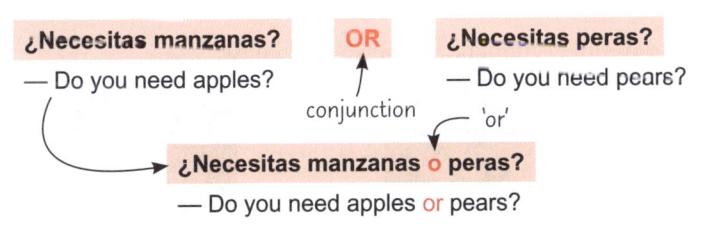

> **¿Necesitas manzanas?** OR **¿Necesitas peras?**
> — Do you need apples?   — Do you need pears?
>   conjunction
>   'or'
> **¿Necesitas manzanas o peras?**
> — Do you need apples or pears?

2) When '<u>o</u>' comes just before a word starting with '<u>o</u>' or '<u>ho</u>', it changes to '<u>u</u>'.

> **Quiero visitar Dinamarca u Holanda.** — I want to visit Denmark or Holland.

Section 6 — Other Useful Stuff

Conjunctions

'Pero' — but

1) 'Pero' means 'but'.

Odio el atún. — I hate tuna.
BUT ← conjunction
Me encanta la merluza. — I love hake.

'but'
Odio el atún pero me encanta la merluza.
— I hate tuna but I love hake.

"I hate you too, Diego."

2) When 'but' means 'but rather', use 'sino'.

No es inglés, sino escocés. — He isn't English, but (rather) Scottish.

'Porque' — because

'Porque' helps you give opinions or explain why something is happening.

'because'
Me gusta mucho esta comida porque es muy picante.
— I really like this food because it's very spicy.

'because'
No puedo venir porque hago de canguro para mis hermanos.
— I can't come because I'm babysitting my siblings.

Other useful conjunctions

Here are some other useful conjunctions you should know.

cuando	when
sin embargo	however
entonces	so

si	if
pues	well / then
como	as / since

a pesar de	despite
incluso	even
así que	therefore

Iremos al cine si llueve mañana. — We will go to the cinema if it rains tomorrow.

Section 6 — Other Useful Stuff

Prepositions

Prepositions help you give information about something's location or time.

Prepositions give extra information

1) Some prepositions tell you where things are in relation to other things in a sentence:

   The dogs are in the garden.

2) Other prepositions tell you when things happen in relation to each other:

   Between April and September.

'A', 'hasta' — to

To say 'to' in Spanish, you normally say 'a', but if 'to' means 'as far as', use 'hasta'.

Vamos a la costa con los nietos. — We're going to the coast with the grandchildren.

Sigue la calle hasta el parque. — Follow the road to (as far as) the park.

'En', 'dentro de' — in

'In' is just 'en' and 'inside' is 'dentro de'. The verb 'entrar' (to go in / to enter) is normally followed by 'en'.

En Londres... — In London...   **dentro de la librería** — inside the bookshop

Entraron en el chalet. — They entered the bungalow.

'De' — of

'De' is usually 'of'. You can also use 'de' to say what something is made of.

You can't say 'de el' or ('a el') in Spanish:

Es de lana. — It's made of wool.

al fondo del armario — at the back of the wardrobe

	el	la
a	al	a la
de	del	de la

Section 6 — Other Useful Stuff

Prepositions

'En', 'a' — at

You can normally use 'en' when you want to say 'at'.
Sometimes you need 'a' instead.

Estamos en el hospital. — We're at the hospital.

a medianoche — at midnight

'Sobre', 'en' — on

For 'on (top of)', use 'sobre' or 'en'. When you mean 'on' but not 'on top of', just use 'en'.

Los platos están sobre la nevera. — The plates are on top of the fridge.

Siempre veo las noticias en la tele. — I always watch the news on TV.

'De', 'desde', 'a partir de' — from

'From' is normally 'de'. Use 'desde' when there's a start and end point and 'a partir de' for dates.

Soy de Bolton. — I'm from Bolton.

desde mayo hasta julio — from May to July

a partir de la semana que viene — from next week

Other common prepositions

Here are some more prepositions you might need.

al lado de	— next to	encima de	— above / on top of
detrás de	— behind	contra	— against
delante de	— in front of	enfrente de	— opposite
entre	— between	al fondo de	— at the back of
bajo / debajo de	— under / below	hacia	— towards

La caja está debajo de tu cama.
— The box is under your bed.

El avión estaba encima de las nubes.
— The plane was above the clouds.

Section 6 — Other Useful Stuff

'Por' and 'Para'

'Por' and 'para' are important prepositions in Spanish. Both of them mean 'for', but don't get caught out — they're not interchangeable...

'Por' — for

Use 'por' to...	Example
...say 'for' in phrases like 'for X years' when you're talking about the past.	Trabajé allí por cuatro años. (I worked there for four years.)
...talk about parts of the day when you want to say 'in'.	por la tarde (in the evening)
...say 'through'.	Corrimos por el bosque. (We ran through the forest.)
...say 'per' or 'a' in number phrases.	cinco veces por año (five times a year)
...talk about exchanges.	Pagué mucho por estos. (I paid a lot for these.)
...say 'on behalf of'.	No lo haré por ti. (I won't do it for you.)
...say 'thank you'.	Gracias por los regalos. (Thank you for the gifts.)

'Para' — for

Use 'para' to...	Example
...say who something is for.	El juguete es para él. (The toy is for him.)
...talk about destinations.	el autobús para Logroño (the bus to Logroño)
...say 'to' or 'in order to'.	Hago ejercicio para mantenerme en forma. (I exercise to keep fit.)
...say 'by' in time phrases.	para el primero de abril (by the first of April)
...say 'for' in phrases like 'for X days' when you're talking about the future.	Me quedo en Madrid para tres días. (I'm staying in Madrid for three days.)
...give an opinion.	Para ella, es demasiado tarde. (For her, it's too late.)
...say 'about to' in the set phrase 'estar para'.	Miguel está para partir. (Miguel is about to leave.)

The personal 'a'

You need an extra 'a' before the word for any human being or pet after every single verb.

You don't usually use the personal 'a' after 'tener' or 'ser'.

He visto a Akame al supermercado. — I saw Akame at the supermarket.

Section 6 — Other Useful Stuff

Index

A
adjectives 19-31
  agreement 20-23
  comparative 30
  demonstrative 19, 27
  indefinite 22, 25
  interrogative 19, 26
  position of 22-24
  possessive 19, 28, 29
  relative 29
  superlative 31
adverbial phrases 32, 35
adverbs 32-37
  comparative 32, 37
  interrogative 34
  of place 34
  of time 34
  superlative 32, 37
articles 2, 5
  definite 2, 5, 6
  indefinite 2, 6
  neuter 5

C
commands 72, 73
comparatives 30, 37
conjunctions 77, 78

D
dates 76
days of the week 76
desde hace 42
desde hacía 50, 55

I
imperatives
    12, 40, 72, 73
infinitives 38, 41
informal and formal 'you'
    9
intensifiers 32, 36

N
negatives 64, 65, 73
nouns 2-4
numbers 75

O
objects 7
ordinal numbers
    22, 23, 75

P
passive 40, 66
personal 'a' 81
plurals 4
por and para 81
prepositions 79, 80
pronouns 7, 72, 73
  demonstrative 7, 18
  interrogative 7, 16
  object 7
    direct 10, 12, 13
    indirect 11-13
    order of 12, 13
  possessive 7, 17
  reflexive 48, 49
  relative 7, 14, 15
  subject 7, 8, 38

Q
quantifiers 32, 36
questions 16, 34, 74
quisiera 40, 71

S
ser and estar 46, 47
stems 42, 44, 53, 60
subjects 38
subjunctive 68-71
  imperfect 40, 71
  present 40, 68, 69, 73
superlatives 19, 31

T
telling the time 76
tenses 39
  conditional 39, 61
  immediate future
    39, 59
  imperfect
    39, 50, 54, 55
  imperfect continuous 63
  perfect 39, 56, 57
  pluperfect 39, 57, 58
  present 39, 42-45, 49
  present continuous
    39, 63
  preterite 39, 50-53
  proper future 39, 60
tú and usted 8, 9

U
un, una 6

V
verbs 38–73
  impersonal 67
  irregular 45, 52, 53,
    55, 57, 62, 69,
    70, 72
  past participles
    56, 57, 66
  present participles
    62, 63
  radical-changing 44
  reflexive 48, 49